LEAD BY DESIGN

APPLYING HUMAN DESIGN PRINCIPLES TO LEADERSHIP STRATEGIES

KRISTIN PANEK

Foreword by
ROBIN WINN

Difference Press

Washington, DC, USA

Published 2022

DISCLAIMER

Cover Design: Kay Moonstar

Editing: Cory Hott

ADVANCE PRAISE

"I truly wish I had read this book years ago. My mantra has always been 'value the differences' and Kristin makes it possible to see how to do that using the powerful tools of Human Design. Leaders do well to listen but intuition without a framework makes it unnecessarily hard. Using real world examples, Kristin walks us through team meetings, work product production and career planning using the invaluable framework of Human Design. The incredible stress and frustration I felt over thirty years of corporate management could have been so different had I had the tools she shares in this gem of a book. The 'aha' moments I had while reading it were many and I will go back to it again and again. I'm thrilled to see it be available to us all."

— PAM MATCHIE-THIEDE, CERTIFIED HUMAN DESIGN PRACTITIONER, FORMER FORTUNE 50 MANAGER: SOFTWARE AND COMMUNICATIONS INDUSTRIES

"Kristin Panek's book, *Lead by Design,* is a game changer on how to attune to your true nature and allow it to emerge organically into thriving leadership. The wonderful thing about her book is that it provided a pathway for me to come home to myself as a leader in my own style and my own flavor. What's so significant about it is that I always thought I had to change myself to be successful. Imagine my delight in discovering that by using my Type, Strategy, and Authority, I already have all the necessary attributes to allow my unique style of leadership to emerge! Kristin's guidance with Human Design, Leadership, and Spirituality is a conductive force which elicits depth, cohesion, and excitement in the journey of discovering one's path as a leader."

— HEIDI WINN, MA, LMHC, CERTIFIED HUMAN
DESIGN COACH

"Kristin Panek's book, *Lead by Design*, gives practical and digestible information that is easy to understand and apply. It expanded my thought process which gave me permission to live unapologetically as an empowered leader. The significant message highlighted how important it will be to live and operate with a defined boundary system based upon our Human Design blueprint which is the key to healthy leadership and success. Through her thought-provoking meditations and contemplations, Kristin's unique approach allows the reader to establish their own direct experience with this technology. Leading based on our strengths by fully embodying our design" is the future of leadership."

— HARMONY PAVETT, OWNER, MANAGING
DIRECTOR, AND SPIRITUAL MENTOR AT
HARMONIC EGG – NAPERVILLE

"Kristin Panek introduces Human Design into leadership in such a way that it induces a burst of inspiration, clarity, and imagination. Throughout reading this gift of a book, I found myself learning new ways of understanding my own design, and the way I want to show up for not only those around me and in my career, but also for *myself* – something that can all too often get neglected as a leader. Kristin has such an innovative way of making the 'intangible' tangible and she does it in a way that will leave you feeling a little lighter and a little better than before you had opened this book."

— MARSTON FRIES, VICE PRESIDENT, SENIOR
ADVISOR CONSULTANT

"*Lead by Design* is for everyone. The book has enough of the basics to allow those not familiar with Human Design to understand the material and how to apply it to themselves while framing the information in new ways that provide ideas for those experienced in Human Design to embody their knowledge. What Kristin does after that is to take the reader deeper. She questions and applies Human Design on a personal level, giving her clients and the reader insights in how to develop a relationship with their design that sets them up for success."

— KELLY RUBY HANSON, AUTHOR OF *DEATH DOULA, TOOLS & TECHNIQUES FOR END OF LIFE SUPPORT*, HUMAN DESIGN PRACTITIONER, DEATH DOULA, AND GRIEF COACH

"Kristin is the leader of a meditation group I have attended for several years. In Kristin's new book, *Lead by Design*, she articulates the Human Design idea so well, backed with real-world examples that I feel as if I have learned a great deal, and was able to apply the teachings to my own chart. This book is meant to be a guide on how to apply the Human Design to your life, and because of Kristin's ability to distill the most important concepts in any topic I believe anyone can apply these teachings to improve their life."

— MIKE HAGGERTY, ACCOUNTING MANAGER

"I think these lines beautifully capture the essence of Kristin Panek's book, *Lead by Design*:

'The truth is this: you're perfectly designed, you carry the qualities you need to succeed, and the world needs you and your unique brand of leadership. When you fully embody your design, you impact situations and people in ways you can't imagine. You inspire others to be their truest and best selves.' In writing *Lead by Design*, Kristin has generously laid out the invitation for me to own and hold every single aspect of my own humanity, and to see all of them and their contradictions for their potential and possibility instead of being problems that need to be fixed. She also provides a blueprint for seeing myself and others in a non-judgmental way, with full curiosity that is both allowing and accepting. This is the most spacious of spaces. I keep discovering that, the more I hold it for myself, the more I'm able to hold it for others. Kristin's gift, her gentle guidance in fostering empathetic leadership through the lens of Human Design could not have arrived at a better time. May it enable all of us to show up as our authentic selves, in full support of one another, as we tackle difficult conversations, tasks, and problems ahead.

—VANESSA QUIROZ, OWNER AND MANAGING
PARTNER OF SYSTEMCORE BUSINESS
SOLUTIONS, BUSINESS DEVELOPMENT AND
HUMAN DESIGN CONSULTANT

"Kristin Panek brings a wise and profound depth of knowledge to the way she embraces and teaches the complexities of Human Design. She is a natural leader who sees your design as your own unique path to greatness. I had the pleasure of Kristin's guidance as I worked my way through Robin Winn's *Foundations of Human Design* Certification course. Kristin has a gift that exemplifies the qualities of true leadership, with the ability to allow her light to shine, as well as becoming a beacon for others to find their gifts through Human Design."

— CINDY CASTILLON, MS, CERTIFIED HUMAN
DESIGN CONSULTANT

"With a blend of intelligent information based on the Human Design model, Kristin's extensive research and personal mystical insights takes us on a journey of self-empowerment in *Lead by Design*. The reader will find a profound message that unlocks leadership gifts hidden due to childhood trauma and also supports the integration of our Awakening process as humanity."

— YOLANDA LOZANO, AUTHOR, SPIRITUAL
GUIDE, SOUND HEALING, FOUNDER OF
HEALING HEARTS

"If you are looking for the best way to step into your leadership, read this book. It will show you your specific path to lead effectively from your strengths, as you get clarity on who you are and your life's purpose."

— SHARON SEABERG NABHAN, EXECUTIVE
LEADERSHIP COACH

"*Lead By Design* offers readers a deep understanding into one's unique power and leadership qualities based on their Human Design. Instead of telling us what to 'fix,' Kristin empowers the reader to more fully understand, embrace, and utilize their distinctive traits to excel in life – regardless of society's projected definition of what leadership 'should' look like. By having their Human Design explained in an easy-to-follow format with Kristin's guidance, the reader is able to really reflect inward without judgment, and to truly embrace and understand the multifaceted diamond of leadership within."

— LEENIE BEE, ER VETERINARY ASSISTANT

"This is the book I've been waiting for. Kristin's exploration of leadership through the lens of Human Design is the soothing antidote to our society's mainstream 'do more, be more' hustle-culture leadership paradigm. Through client stories and beautiful meditations, Kristin guides us gracefully back home to ourselves, our design and our unique gifts so we can make the impact we are craving in the world. This book is for humans who want their leadership to be rooted in the sacred truth of who they are."

— NATTY FRASCA, FOUNDER OF *THE FEMININE REBELLION*, FEMININE LEADERSHIP AND PLEASURE COACH

CONTENTS

To my grandson Jack, who arrived on the last supermoon of 2022 and captured my heart
May you realize your magnificence and lead your life by being unapologetically you.

FOREWORD

Are you a leader? Some of us are clearly called to leadership. Others of us have to be cajoled or required to step into leadership. Others still are the quiet leaders whose roles are rarely recognized. From a Human Design perspective, the question is not *whether you are a leader,* but *in what ways are you a leader?*

How does your leadership reveal itself? Are you allowing it? Is there a way to align with your natural leadership, to step into your power? How do you best lead? Are you able to call others into their leadership capacities? Can Human Design help you take your leadership to the next level? In *Lead by Design: Applying Human Design Principles to Leadership Strategies,* Kristin Panek takes you on a journey to step into your full potential as a leader.

I first met Kristin in The Author Incubator, where she had been writing books on leadership while I was writing books on Human Design. At the time she had published two books, *Authentic Leadership: The Guide to be a Spiritual Leader in Your Community* and *My Family Needs My Spiritual Leadership Now: The*

Guide to Being Your Family's Spiritual Support. I had published *Understanding Your Clients through Human Design: The Breakthrough Technology* and was completing my second book *Understanding the Centers in Human Design: The Facilitator's Guide to Transforming Pain into Possibility.* My third book *Understanding the Profiles in Human Design: The Facilitator's Guide to Unleashing Potential* was still in the conception phase. While we knew of each other's work and were part of a larger community of authors, we didn't really connect personally until she interviewed me to introduce her community to Human Design.

Kristin presents with an adventurous openness combined with a stable, grounded, understated demeanor. She admittedly knew very little about Human Design. In the interview I asked if it was ok, as a way of introducing her to Human Design, if I said a few things about her chart; she was totally game. As I reflected the information from the chart she listened with a rare quality of attentive stillness. I watched as a flurry of emotion welled up and threw her off guard. Incredulous, she was being reflected in an unexpected and disarming way. It was lovely – and gratifying – to experience how deeply she grokked the Human Design system as it applied to her life. At the same time, she registered the potential impact Human Design could have through supporting others.

As we finished our interview, it was clear Kristin had been deeply affected, and that the trajectory of her life was about to change. She was taken, ready to embark on a new adventure. She signed up on the spot to join the Human Design Certification Training for Professionals that was starting that month. Fully committed, all in, Kristin imbibed the teachings and immediately started using Human Design in both her personal and professional lives. A clear leader, she went on to assist in the certification trainings, as well as supporting me in workshops and trainings I offered to businesses. Her unassuming steady ground and insightful wisdom were a powerful ballast, consistently adding a depth and richness to the trainings and events.

When it came time for her to write this third book, Kristin had been steeped in Human Design and woven its potent teachings into her work empowering leaders. Her obvious next offering was to bring her passion for leadership together with her appreciation and understanding of Human Design. Aligned with her design, Kristin was ready to inspire leaders to claim their sovereignty and gain a new level of insight into how others operate.

Lead by Design is a masterful weaving of Kristin's deep insight into the process of transformation and the powerful reflection Human Design offers to leaders. Skillfully using stories of leaders grappling with real life issues she points to the challenges they face and how understanding their chart can bring new ways to approach their difficulties. With the story of Maggie, we are drawn into the world of a clearly powerful leader who is frustrated by her lack of impact. Throughout the book we watch as Maggie learns her design, why she has the challenges she has, how she's been operating out of alignment with her design, and what happens when she does align. (I'll leave you to read about it...)

With a keen understanding of leaders and their challenges, Kristin lays out a path to help you use Human Design to see who you truly are, clear limiting patterns and beliefs that are not yours, and proceed to claim your dream. When you step into Kristin's world you are called to turn away from the ocean of *shoulds* and expectations that bog down your brilliance and instead open to your inner guidance. You are invited to claim your sovereignty and own your unique leadership path.

With Kristin as your wise and worthy guide, and as a well-travelled companion on the transformational path, know that you will be led to go deeper in yourself so you can go outward more powerfully and effectively.

Walk confidently with Kristin on the journey to open to and honor your leadership potential.

— ROBIN WINN, MFT, NOVEMBER 25, 2022,

MAUI, HAWAII

LEVERAGING YOUR HUMAN DESIGN TO BE A BETTER LEADER

When someone fully embodies who they are, they become the type of leader they're meant to be, which may not fit traditional cultural ideals. A leader understands their natural strengths, how they influence people and situations, and how they achieve success. They set a direction and follow it. People naturally follow them, and that leader brings out the best in others along the way.

Too many people are caught up in the chaos and unpredictability of this world, letting it influence them rather than leading their lives in the direction they choose. Some begin to doubt their leadership. Maybe you've had moments of doubt about your ability to have an impact. Perhaps you've strayed off course, buying into fear or a sense of hopelessness, inadequacy, or false superiority. There are universal beliefs sitting in the collective consciousness: "I'm not good enough," "They should respect me," "I'm right," "I can't make a mistake," "I need to know," "I should have more energy," "I should be more decisive," "I'm a fraud." It's easy to latch on to one of these themes, wrap a story around it, and mistake it for your belief. This can happen without you realizing it. Then you find yourself spiraling down into more negativity, perhaps believing that you can't change it or improve your situation. You've just abandoned yourself.

The truth is this: you're perfectly designed, you carry the qualities you need to succeed, and the world needs you and your unique brand of leadership. When you fully embody your design, you impact situations and people in ways you can't imagine. You inspire others to be their truest and best selves.

Whether you are embarking on a path of leadership in the arena of business, relationships, health or spirituality, Human Design can shed light on your purpose as well as your gifts and challenges. It can light the way to you stepping into your full power as a leader. If you dream of making an impact in the world, you can do it!

ARE YOU A LEADER?

Are you questioning your call to leadership or your current leadership role?

Maybe you're like my client Maggie who is reevaluating her relationship to work and to her home life.

Maybe you've been naturally called into leadership and yet doubted yourself and your capacities. Maybe you've heard about Human Design, and it sparked a curiosity. Maybe you're looking for new leadership strategies to take your work to the next level.

Let's take a closer look at Maggie's story and see if there are elements of it that resonate with you.

Maggie had recently returned from driving her daughter to school in New York and had plenty of time on the drive home to Chicago to think about her current circumstance. A friend had told her about Human Design and how it changed the way she made decisions and how she related with family and coworkers. Maggie had noticed that her friend seemed more at peace with herself. Maggie longed for that sense of peace and wondered if Human Design could help her.

When I first met Maggie, she told me, "I have always been placed in leadership positions and people value my opinions. I have what it takes to be good leader, and yet I don't always believe that about myself. I still struggle with it so much day to day."

I wish I could say that people called to leadership are naturally confident, at ease, comfortable with their skills, and believe in themselves. But the truth is people in leadership struggle just like everyone else.

In Maggie's case, it was clear that people like working for her because she's honest with them and lets them know what's going on in the company. She loves her team members, yet she often finds it easier to do the work than to delegate. Her boss wants her to fix this issue but doesn't press the point because she effectively manages a large workload and meets her deadlines. Maggie tends to keep to herself at work. Other managers meet for drinks afterward, but she has always needed to pick up her kids or drive them to activities. Even though her kids are now grown and gone, she still has little desire to socialize after work. As a result, she often receives feedback about not being a team player, although senior managers keep putting her on teams. They know about her huge capacity to juggle many projects successfully. Because Maggie moves quickly, she sometimes makes mistakes, and her peers are quick to point it out in meetings. She runs proposals and project updates by managers in her organization who are good with details, but she can't share everything with them. She believes her colleagues are envious that she's assigned to more high-profile projects.

Maggie was particularly frustrated about some recent changes at work, which brought her to me.

"I know I'm a good leader, but I feel like I have shortcomings that are holding me back. I've tried to work on slowing down and being more careful, but I just get frustrated and still make mistakes. I've tried to delegate more. But then it takes more time, and I feel low on patience. I try to be the kind of leader the company values – decisive, confident, communicative – but sometimes I'm anxious about making quick decisions. I've been passed over for two promotions lately despite my accomplishments. They brought in high-level managers from the outside to fill the positions. I'm missing something, but I don't know what or where to look for it."

She continued, "I feel like I've been running on high speed my entire life – getting through college and graduate school while raising a family and working full time. I've always just jumped in and done what I knew to do. While our company offers leadership trainings, I don't feel like they are speaking to me. I tune out the trainer and answer work emails during the classes. I've done well and have been recognized with good bonuses. Now that my kids are in college, I have some free time to look at my life and make some changes. I would like to know what I don't know about myself. What's stopping me from being more successful and feeling fulfilled?"

Hearing Maggie's story, I nodded and smiled, noticing how much we had in common. Maggie was one of my early Human Design clients, and I marveled at the way the Universe sent me the perfect clients for my learning at the time.

She went on to tell me that her ideas are not appreciated. She'd like to bring new ways of hiring and training people into her organization, but her boss is not interested in hearing new ideas. He's busy trying to gain respect from other department heads. He doesn't want to rock the boat, and he relies heavily on her expertise. He wants her focused on producing. He doesn't have time to consider implementing new procedures. Every time she brings it up his eyes glaze over. Then Maggie begins to doubt herself. At other times, Maggie believes she needs to be promoted so she will have enough influence to express her ideas and to receive senior management support.

As Maggie spoke I thought about her Human Design chart. No surprise – everything she said was reflected in her chart. Maggie's Human Design shows she is here to take a leadership role, especially in situations that need change. She is completely in tune with her mission but frustrated and angry when her solutions are ignored. Her design also shows a tremendous capacity to juggle many projects and generate more work in a couple hours than most people generate in a day. She's designed to see potential improvements, voice her ideas in the right timing, and impact people and situations.

From Maggie's perspective, a good leader communicates effectively and takes initiative. But in her experience when she spoke her ideas and initiated action, she kept hitting roadblocks. Something was off.

Maggie had already left one company earlier in her career because her ideas about improving processes and structures were often not well received. While she was doing better in her current situation, this pattern of difficulty with introducing change still periodically repeated itself. She was mystified until we looked at her Human Design Type and Strategy and she discovered that she actually needs to be in response rather than initiate. Surprised and skeptical yet tired of hitting a brick wall with her ideas, she was open to changing her approach.

As I shared more elements of her Human Design, Maggie resonated with the emphasis on leadership in her chart. People always recognize that in her. Still, seeing it in the chart had a big impact. She realized that her struggles were not due to her leadership ability but rather to an ineffective communication style that didn't match her Human Design. She had been sharing her ideas for the company before it was appropriate and making decisions when she was on an emotional high. If she were to follow her Human Design Authority, she would need to come to a place of stillness for more clarity. She saw that being a bit pushy when trying to get her points across was contrary to her design. Based on her chart, Maggie is also here to support others in accessing their Inner Authority. Trying to shortcut the process by powering her ideas through would cost her and her team in the long run.

Maggie was also relieved to hear that with her tremendous capacity and speed came a propensity to skip steps. This was not a weakness but part of her design. Slowing down was not the answer. She was built for high productivity and needed to inform her team, so they could look for any missing steps and let her know. She also realized that not everyone has her high workload capacity and speed. She resolved to stop expecting that type of output from her team. They had felt her high expectations for them and her disappointment when they didn't meet that high bar. They were frustrated too.

Maggie began to integrate her understanding of her Human Design chart and was already noticing the impact at work. As she relaxed the standards she had imposed on the team, they felt more accepted and became more productive. As she moved deeper in her understanding of Human Design, she stopped making assumptions and worked to be more present and aware.

Maggie's experience of herself began to shift. She felt more confidence and trust in herself. She discovered how to leverage her design to enhance her communication skills. Eventually her boss listened to her ideas and sent them to the senior management team who was willing to investigate them further. New opportunities came from operating in alignment with her design. Maggie didn't need to change who she was. Instead she needed effective strategies to work with her design.

GETTING CLARITY

What are you struggling with in your leadership role? What if, like Maggie, there is nothing you need to change to be a better leader? Maybe it's not about improving yourself but rather a journey of becoming clearer about how you're wired and how to optimize that. What if you could call off the quest to shore up your weak points or to get more pointers on how to be a better leader?

If you've picked up this book, something inside of you is nudging you to further open to that natural leader in you. You don't have to be at the effect of others' expectations or plans for you. You can fully embrace who you are, unlocking the brilliant gifts you carry and walk through the world in a way that encourages others to do the same.

From the Human Design perspective, each one of us is perfectly designed. Each one of us has a unique light to illuminate the world.

Are you ready to let your light shine?

2

HUMAN DESIGN: UNLOCKING THE MISSING PIECE OF LEADERSHIP CHALLENGES

"You're here to save the world," Robin said to me matter-of-factly. Several different expressions ran across my face as I responded internally. "How does she know? And doesn't that sound grandiose to say out loud? It rings true. Wow. Maybe I'm not crazy to think this way."

This was my introduction to Human Design.

I was interviewing Robin Winn on Facebook Live to help promote her first book, *Understanding Your Clients Through Human Design: The Breakthrough Technology*. I lost control of the "interview" within the first few minutes as she neatly laid out all my conundrums, gifts, and challenges. I was melting down internally, and I was hooked. How is it possible that all of this is in a chart based on my time, date and city of birth?

I had heard about Human Design for years but had consciously avoided it. I didn't need another modality to add to my list of certifications. I was a little skeptical anyway about anything that showed a person's traits and challenges and wondered whether it would be useful with my teams.

I've been thrust into leadership positions since I was young, at times reluctantly. As captain of our Varsity volleyball team in college, working with an encouraging coach, I started owning that leader in me. In the early years of my business career, when I tried to remain in the background or out of the line of fire, I ended up giving presentations to the president of our company. Directly after college, I started my career as a manager of econometrics, then later moved into corporate strategy at Ameritech, and next into a director of pricing at Ameritech Cellular. I was often given special projects where I was working directly with the president and leading teams to evaluate or implement innovative ideas.

Robin explained that based on my design, I'm here to support leaders to help them realize their big dreams, within the context of whatever limitations they're experiencing. I'm here to support them in creating a new leadership story for themselves and to live into that. A deep *yes* welled up within me. Time stopped. I was standing in the truth of who I was. Robin gave me a moment to be with the new insights that were flowing through me.

It's not that I didn't know these things. I had, after all, written two books on Leadership – *Authentic Leadership: The Guide to Be a Spiritual Leader in Your Community* and *My Family Needs My Spiritual Leadership Now: The Guide to Being Your Family's Spiritual Support.*

I was an experienced leader in both the corporate and spiritual worlds. I was a general manager at Ameritech with six hundred people in my organization when I left to follow a new dream – one I didn't know yet but was quietly tugging at my heart. I simply knew that after twenty years, it was time to go. Surprisingly, I ended up building spiritual communities and spending the next twenty-five years guiding and supporting leaders in this realm. I studied at Oneness University in India and eventually founded Flowering Heart Center, to shift consciousness and empower people to realize their big dreams, work through their limitations, and create new stories for themselves. But the reflection, the validation, and the revelation that this was actually my blueprint, opened a new level of permission to fully claim and live who I knew myself to be. It was exactly this capacity to reveal what was clearly true all along that was the missing key for myself and my clients.

As I shared Human Design with my clients, they found a renewed appreciation of who they were and a sense of empowerment about claiming that. Using Human Design, they came to understand how to follow their guidance and make better decisions.

But I'm getting ahead of myself.

OTHER ASSESSMENT SYSTEMS

During the mid-nineties, Myers Briggs was gaining popularity. The president of Ameritech Cellular brought in a consultant to test mid- and upper-level managers so we could understand each other better. I was excited to learn more about myself, my coworkers, and my teams. My results showed what I already knew – that my personality type was an introvert with a strategic, logical way of thinking that likes to focus on abstract information rather than concrete details. This left me with a lot of questions.

While the information about my work colleagues was helpful, it didn't change how I interacted with them. I could acknowledge our differences, but I didn't receive any specific instructions on how to interface with them more effectively. And I became disillusioned when I saw how people manipulated the test.

It was a well-known fact within the company that the president loved people who were outgoing and strong. When my boss took the Myers Briggs test, she answered the questions as if she was an extrovert, despite the fact that she had admitted she was an introvert. Most of these assessments, such as DISC, depend on people answering a set of questions. Even when employees answer to the best of their ability, their responses are often from their conditioning rather than their true selves.

All of us take on beliefs, especially as young children, from our family of origin or our teachers and friends. We're not aware that these beliefs are not ours until they're seen and questioned. These beliefs, meanwhile, are like programs running in our subconscious, coloring the lens through which we see the world. The answers we give to assessment questions are being filtered through those beliefs.

I appreciate that companies recognize people have different ways of operating and are striving to learn more about their employees. Those were some of the best tools available at the time, but I would have liked a tool that was free from biases and didn't depend on someone answering a list of questions. Astrology can support, but it seemed so complicated, and I wasn't drawn to study it.

HUMAN DESIGN – THE NEW ASSESSMENT TOOL

When I listened to Robin as she laid out my internal wiring based on my birth information, I was floored and fascinated by the possibilities. She pointed to areas within me where conditioning is likely to land and how to work with that. I knew in that moment why I had avoided Human Design for so many years – I wasn't ready to receive it because I didn't have room in my life to study it deeply. My design loves to delve into information. But this was the tool I had been wanting.

Human Design was originally downloaded into a reluctant mystic named Ra in 1987. He was told that this information was for everyone but especially important for parents to support their children. Understanding their children's blueprint could help parents see their children for who they were and know how to help them thrive. Based on ancient technologies such as astrology, the I Ching, and the Kabbalah, as well as newer understanding from quantum physics, Human Design is a new application. It recognizes the innate brilliance and perfection of each person, as well as the challenges they may face. This quintessential guide is a map - a blueprint - for our potential. Multifaceted, the Human Design chart is looking at our operating system. It classifies humanity into five Types, each with its ideal Strategy for succeeding in life. It also shows each person's unique Authority, or decision-making process, as well as their Profile, or learning style. There are more pieces or layers – including Gates, Channels, the Planets – each revealing layers of understanding of who we are and how we navigate the world.

After my experience with Robin, I signed up for her training and began my journey with Human Design. I was completely taken in by it. The information grabbed hold of me, and I received downloads as I looked at charts. Fully engaged, I generated charts of my family and friends, marveling at their accuracy. At one point I ran the chart of my friend Yolanda and found myself exclaiming, "That's not Yolanda." I was a little shocked at myself – how did I know this? I was relatively new to this modality, but I trusted my intuition and called her about her birth time. She said she was born in an ambulance on the way to the hospital, so her actual time was likely earlier than 5:00 a.m. After asking her a few questions, I landed on 4:48 as her birth time.

Now, after working with over a hundred clients, not one person has said "This doesn't sound like me." Most of them tell me that they feel truly seen and acknowledged. Human Design has been the missing link for me in my work with leaders. I often wished I had a window into how people operated while managing teams in the business world and then later in the spiritual world. Since I've discovered Human Design my work with them has gone to a whole new level.

REVELATIONS ABOUND

Learning about my design and how I operate resolved some inner conflict inside of me. I see this again and again with my clients as well. True to my design as a Manifesting Generator, I excel at multitasking and juggling many big projects at once. The corporate world has gone back and forth on the merits of multitasking, judging whether it's a good or bad idea. They now warn that it can actually slow you down to work on multiple things at once. People used to tell me to slow down, do one thing at a time, and I tried unsuccessfully. Now I know that I'm built for speed and capacity and no longer feel guilty about this gift. Every time I move something off my plate, something else comes on it. I don't have to make myself wrong anymore.

I am careful to follow my Inner Authority about what goes on my list of projects. At the time I said *yes* to writing this book, I was training to walk the Portuguese El Camino, moving out of the physical space in which our spiritual center is located, starting to teach a five-week online leadership course, and preparing to go to Denver for the birth of my grandson. It seemed impossible to add writing a book to this list, but I trusted my inner *yes*. I've been criticized for attempting so many things at once, especially when I skip steps. It's my nature, and an alchemical process occurs when several major projects are due at once. Something magical always happens. The various projects usually inform each other, making them more successful. Part of my spiritual journey has been learning to trust and surrender to the process. I was happy to have it confirmed in my Human Design.

In that initial interview with Robin, she talked about people projecting on me, both positively and negatively. I've experienced that and tend to hide from it, showing who I am to a smaller group of people. My Profile or learning style, is the most transpersonal of all twelve Profiles. I'm here to take knowledge and make it beneficial in a universal way. People sense that I have something they need and when the timing is right, I enjoy playing the savior with my incredible problem-solving capacity. If my timing is wrong or I haven't done my research, and I can't carry through, I become the heretic. Looking back on my life, I could relate to this too. Also included in my design, is the ability to look at past patterns and bring solutions to the tribe that help them thrive. When the tribe is not interested, I become disheartened.

At the time of the interview with Robin, I was sitting with a big decision to leave Shematrix mystery school after twenty-one years with them. I was a member of their senior leadership team and a vital community member helping to grow this collective. I'd been getting internal signals to leave for a few months and had been completing projects in preparation to go. But a part of me didn't want to let go. Thoughts were tugging at me trying to keep me safe: "You can't go... What about your sisters and your community?" I continued quietly making my plans, determined to ignore the thoughts. Robin immediately went to that part of the chart, "You're not meant to be in maintenance mode. You're here to bring change, and then step out when your guidance tells you." In that moment, I felt validated, and then a huge release of energy. Light filled my heart. I'm not crazy to leave... Permission to leave...

She also pointed to a basic tension in my chart between working alone and with a team, mentioning that I'm meant to do both. I was recalling all the comments I had received about being too independent. I realized that by trying to improve the parts of me that I thought were "wrong," I was not honoring my design or leveraging my strengths. My independence, speed and capacity are strengths, as well as my ability to learn from the past and bring innovative solutions, to realize big dreams, and to work within limitations.

I felt seen and validated. I didn't need to change. I needed to focus on my strengths and inform others about how I operate so they could adjust. Seeing it clearly in my chart gave me the confidence to do that. My journey with Human Design also gave me an appreciation of how others are wired and strategies to meet them where they're at. I see the beauty in each person's design and help them fully embody it.

Sometimes the leaders I support are initially a little dismayed when they find out how they are wired. "You mean I need to wait to be invited to speak? I can't share my brilliant ideas unless someone is asking?" When they understand that based on their design, they're already impacting the room by their presence, they begin to relax into the wise guide that they are designed to be.

Our culture places such a high value on communication, decisiveness, and confidence, which is often about making decisions in the moment. These are among the most common desires with which leaders come to me. Most people are not wired to decide in the moment. They need time to become clear or to integrate the information they're taking in. If forced to decide quickly, that decision will be a conditioned response and not come from their wisdom and experience. Everyone loses.

I am wired to make decisions in the moment and couldn't understand why my partner was not able to do this. I would watch him take in information and consider it for a while, wondering what was going on in there. Now I understand his design and give him that time he needs to come to a decision.

When he does, it's well considered, and he can explain his process and reasoning in great detail. This has been a healing balm in our relationship.

IT'S TIME TO STEP INTO LEADERSHIP

The world needs strong leaders right now with the ability to meet people where they are, instead of placing them into categories based on their beliefs. Many people are currently operating out of fear and according to other people's rules, disconnected from their internal guidance. They're leading out of alignment with their design. This is the cause of a lot of burnout and disillusionment. People are truly beautifully diverse in how they operate and in their strengths. To be able to see, appreciate, and work with this is one of the big gifts of Human Design.

Everyone's design is perfect. Rather than focusing on "weaknesses," it's time to support leaders to more deeply embody their designs, lead from a place of strength, and trust their decision-making process. My work is to help leaders live their designs, clarify goals, and move toward them so they can lead in all aspects of their life instead of being at the effect of external events and circumstances. When people operate from this place, they can succeed even if their company culture values a different design.

As previously mentioned, I have spent over twenty years in the corporate world in leadership positions and over twenty years in the spiritual development world, creating and leading communities. I'm well versed in how to support people to be successful in life, to face their fears, to release sabotaging beliefs, to lead from their strengths. This is my calling. I am here to help leaders develop trust and a deep connection to their inner guidance. With a wide range of tools, I support people to meet their challenges. With Human Design, I can see their whole operating system at a glance, focus in quickly on the areas of potential conundrums, and offer specific guidance based on their wiring.

I'm writing this just a couple of days after returning from the birth of my first grandbaby, Jack. He arrived in this world after a long and difficult journey at the peak of the full supermoon in August. As I first held him in my arms, I was in awe of this newborn, who is beautiful, whole, and perfect. Despite his vulnerable state, all of his needs are met. He is fully himself and this is part of his charm. His rational mind has not yet come online to tell him what he should be, where he needs *fixing*, or that he doesn't measure up to some perceived ideal.

I was honored to be there at his birth. Since I was able to capture the exact time, I could look at his Human Design and get a sense of this deep soul. Then I remembered holding my children for the first time, wishing desperately for some kind of manual to tell me how to parent them. It turns out that both of my children have a learning Profile in which they need to gather information first and then learn by trial and error. People with this learning style rarely seek advice because they're built to figure things out on their own. As a young mother, I felt helpless because my children didn't want my input. I thought it was my issue – that what I had to say wasn't worthwhile. Had I known this is how my children are designed, I could have relaxed more in my mothering style.

Jack is fortunate, because his parents will have some insights into how to best support his unique and powerful design as a Projector. You'll learn more about what parenting support he needs when we cover the various Types in Chapter 5. Jack's many gifts can be nurtured through an understanding of himself and how to effectively interact with others.

3

ORIENTING YOURSELF TO THIS JOURNEY

You're embarking on a journey that will likely change the way you look at life and how you navigate it. I'm excited to be your guide because I know what's possible. You're about to take your leadership to the next level and the size of that step is as big as you want it to be. I know you're ready to dive in. I'll give you a short itinerary so you can orient yourself to the program.

Leading by Design starts in Chapter 4 with a simple overview of your Human Design chart to introduce you to this system. If you're already aware of those concepts, this will be a high-level review. You can also use this chapter as a reference as you read through the rest of the book.

In Chapter 5, you'll get a basic understanding of the five different Human Design Types so that you can begin to align with your Type, Strategy, and Authority. If you've already had a session with a professional to review your chart, that will be helpful. If not, this will provide some valuable points for you, and enough information to follow the Lead by Design steps. It's important to have a basic understanding of the wiring or your vehicle before you start driving toward your destination.

In Chapter 6, we'll briefly step beyond Human Design to incorporate and learn about what I call the World Design, and how to align with that. When you are aware of the world mirror and the impact of that reflection field, you'll move more consciously and efficiently toward your goals.

Chapter 7 will support you in determining a destination. You may already have some goals, but this is a chance to look at the bigger picture and perhaps revisit them. Your Human Design will provide a high-level view and a useful starting point for this exploration. If you don't yet have specific goals, it's important to choose where you're headed, rather than letting the winds of chance blow you around or, worse, being led by other people's agendas and power trips.

In Chapter 8, you'll recognize that even though you're moving in the direction you've chosen, roadblocks and detours are inevitable. You'll learn about the most common ones so that you can steer clear. You'll also learn what to do if you detour off the road into a cornfield maze and can't find your way out.

Chapter 9 will draw you deeper into your Human Design to discover some of your gifts and vulnerabilities. You'll learn more about the nine Centers and some characteristics of Open and Defined Centers. This information can also be used for reference as you read through the book. You'll discover conditioning or patterns in your Centers where you've taken on other peoples' ideas as your own. You'll learn how to release those ideas and leverage your design for more success.

In Chapter 10, you'll increase your effectiveness through learning how to control your attention. You have two main levers to create your reality – intention and attention. You'll work with focusing on your inner and outer world at the same time, so you can be aware and able to respond appropriately. Then you'll have an opportunity to clarify your leadership style and create your person credo by which to live.

In Chapter 11, you'll take what you've learned about your design and look at how you might support others more effectively. By now you have some appreciation of how differently each person operates. To inspire and motivate them, you'll learn to engage in various specific conversations to understand their viewpoints.

Chapter 12 talks about your journey going forward and identifies areas where you may like support to stay on track.

By Chapter 13 you'll have an appreciation of what's possible with this Lead by Design process. You'll know how to align with your design, claim who you are and lead effectively from your strengths.

I've guided leaders through this Lead by Design process, and more recently I led myself through it. When my friend Dawn asked me to walk the Portuguese El Camino, my response was "Yes!" We had walked the French Camino three years earlier, so I knew I was in for an intense and rewarding experience. Unlike last time, I was very familiar with my Human Design and knew how to align with it so that I had sustainable energy. I also had a new appreciation for why I'm drawn to this pilgrimage. My spiritual path lies in the Gate of Struggle, which is why the El Camino walk aligns perfectly with my design. It's a good struggle, one that is well worth my total commitment and energy.

This time I packed lightly because I trusted that I would be taken care of, and the world reflected that back to me. Each day as I walked out the door, I reaffirmed that I would be supported in all ways, and I committed to following my Inner Authority. Almost every day we received help in various surprising ways. For example, one afternoon we passed by a beautiful hostel about five miles outside of town and decided to stop inside to ask for a stamp for our Pilgrim Credentials. We'd never stopped inside other hostels just to check them out, but our guidance was leading us there. As the manager stamped our credentials, we noticed our bags were on the floor behind her desk! This was not our destination. Seeing our shock, the manager graciously offered to send our bags ahead to our destination in town, and we gratefully continued our journey.

On another day, we received some much-needed clothing. One of my two T-shirts had a hole in it, and Dawn had lost one of her two pairs of hiking socks. We arrived one night to an apartment where someone had left behind a T-shirt in my size and a pair of socks for Dawn – the specific brand she wears for hiking! We graciously accepted these gifts.

Each day's destination was about fifteen miles away, up and down hills in hot weather. Every morning, I visualized us reaching our destination and then consciously let go of focusing on it, because that led to too much suffering. Instead, I learned to sink into the joy of walking in nature and through ancient villages. Yes, I experienced pain with all the stresses on the body, but I didn't focus on that problem. Instead, I focused on the healing effects of movement. I let go of negativity and fear, and kept directing my attention both inside myself (to make sure I was walking in correct form) and simultaneously outside myself (looking for yellow marker arrows and rocks that might trip me). In this way I could respond appropriately to the unexpected. It's easy to get lost in thoughts and start walking in the wrong direction. It's also easy to have too much attention on the outside, looking for yellow trail marker arrows, and overriding potential body issues. I was constantly reminded to keep my focus on both. This ability to direct attention is invaluable for reaching goals and experiencing success in life. On this trip, I had thirty days of constant practice.

I had to let go of comparison – there was always someone faster and stronger. I had to let go of my idea of what the Camino should look like. For example, just outside of Lisbon there were few places to get water or shelter from the hot sun. The yellow arrows were not always easy to find, and there were a lot of cobblestone streets, which are hard on the feet.

I kept letting go and directing my attention in the moment, responding to my guidance. The journey became joyful. The world took care of me in creative ways, helping me reach my daily goals. Long before I finished the four-hundred-mile walk, I felt a profound sense of inner peace that is still with me. It comes partly from a deep knowing that I'm always taken care of if I allow it (even in the middle of rural Spain).

This is possible for you too. Following the steps in this Lead by Design process will bring you a sense of contentment and joy, as well as greater success in your endeavors. You'll marvel at the way the Universe conspires to bring you what you need. And you don't have to wait until you've reached your goal; you can experience joy in the journey as you take your leadership to another level. I realized the transformative nature of this process as I walked across Portugal and Spain.

The steps in this book are deceptively powerful. Use a journal, track your progress, record your insights, and celebrate wins. New habits and skills take time to develop, but it's worth the commitment of time and energy.

You can change your world. You cannot imagine right now the power you wield. You can't imagine your magnificence.

Observe.

Practice.

Trust.

It works.

4

A SIMPLE OVERVIEW OF YOUR HUMAN DESIGN CHART

L et's start with a basic orientation to your Human Design chart, so you can be prepared to align more closely with your leadership style. Go get your chart before you read any further. This link: http://www.leadbyde signwithkristin.com/bodygraph will take you to a web page that will generate your chart.

Refer to your chart or the bodygraph below (Chart A).

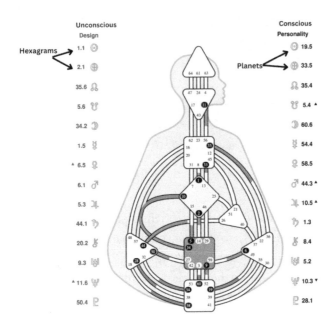

Unconscious
Design

Hexagrams

1.1 ☉
2.1 ⊕
35.6 ♌
5.6 ♋
34.2 ☽
1.5 ☿
▲ 6.5 ♀
6.1 ♂
5.3 ♃
44.1 ♄
20.2 ⛢
9.3 ♆
▲ 11.6 ♇
50.4 ♇

Conscious
Personality

Planets

☉ 19.5
⊕ 33.5
♌ 35.4
♋ 5.4 ▲
☽ 60.6
☿ 54.4
♀ 58.5
♂ 44.3 ▲
♃ 10.5 ▲
♄ 1.3
⛢ 8.4
♆ 5.2
♇ 10.3 ▼
♇ 28.1

Looking at your chart might evoke a sense of curiosity, or it might trigger a sense of overwhelm, due to its complexity. You may also recognize some of the Human Design elements, which include astrology and the traditional Hindu chakra system, as well as the I Ching, the Kabbalah, and quantum physics. All these elements work together to bring you a deeply informative manual on your unique operating system.

It's beyond the scope of this book to explain the entirety of this system, but understanding the bigger influences in your chart can have life-altering impact on your leadership capacities. Let's start your orientation with the most prominent and fundamental aspects of the chart: Type, Strategy, and Authority. Then we'll briefly look at the Centers, Definition and Openness, the Channels, Gates, Planets and I Ching, the Profiles, Definition, and finally the Incarnation Cross. If you're new to this modality, it may be a lot to take in, but if you look at your chart while reading this material, it will begin to ground the information. Also, throughout the book, I'll refer to the elements in the chart as I tell stories about clients on their leadership path. In that way you'll get a sense of how the chart information can support you to step into your full power as a leader.

TYPE

Human Design groups people into five fundamentally different Types. Each Type has its own gifts and challenges although our culture may currently prize certain traits over others. All designs are needed to make society operate effectively. The issues are NOT related to which Type you happen to be, but rather to living out of alignment with yourself, which can create needless obstacles. The five Human Design Types are Generators, Manifesting Generators, Manifestors, Projectors, and Reflectors. Each of these Types operate differently. Again, to be clear, there is no hierarchy in Human Design. Each Type has an important function and contribution. I'll go deeper into the Five Types later in the chapter, but for now, here is an initial introduction to them.

Generators make up 35 percent of humanity. They have sustainable energy and are here to find their right work. Another 35 percent of humanity are Manifesting Generators. Like Generators they have sustainable energy and are here to find their right work. In addition, Manifesting Generators are here to impact humanity. They empower the people around them by their mere presence. Manifestors, often referred to as The Generals, make up 8 percent of humanity. Lacking the sustainable energy of the Generators and Manifesting Generators, the self-possessed Manifestors have a big force field and are here to impact the direction of life. Projectors are 21 percent of humanity. They're here to be the wise guides, directing the energy rather than generating energy. Finally, the rare and unusual Reflectors make up 1 percent of the population. They're here to mirror the health, or lack of health, in the communities they inhabit.

STRATEGY

Each Type has what we call a specific Strategy, an optimal way of functioning in life. For example, The Generator Strategy is to be in response to life. Generators are here to follow their *yeses* and *noes*. Their yes/no response is their inner GPS and allows them to optimize their power and master life. The Manifesting Generator, like the Generator also has the Strategy to be in response to life following their inner GPS, their *yeses* and *noes* in order to master life. However, to fully step into their power they also have the Strategy to inform. Before they initiate, they'll have a bigger impact if they first let people know what they're going to do. Manifestors are here to impact the world. Lacking the inner GPS, they realize their strength by informing before they act. Projectors are here to be the wise guides of humanity. Theirs is one of the more challenging Strategies as far as cultural norms and conditioning. Projectors get their best results when they wait for an invitation that feels good to them or are recognized before they speak. Finally, the unusual Reflectors have a Strategy of waiting over time (it's often said they need to wait a full lunar cycle) before they make decisions.

Look at your chart, identify your Type and Strategy, and contemplate. Do your Type and Strategy resonate? Or perhaps you notice you're not living in alignment with your chart. Are you initiating when you're designed to be in response? Maybe you're trying to generate when the best use of your energy is to guide.

AUTHORITY

Along with Type and Strategy, each person has an optimal way of making decisions, called Authority. At the simplest level there are four kinds of Authority: Emotional, Sacral, Splenic, and No Authority.

If you have Emotional Authority, your best form of decision-making is over time, after you've had a chance to see if what you're planning to do feels good to you. If you have Sacral Authority, you're designed to make decisions in the moment, following your *yeses* and *noes* (understanding that more information might change your response). If you have Splenic Authority you're designed to follow your intuition. If your chart says any other Authority, we'll refer to it here as "No Authority," and you'll need to listen to yourself speak in order to decide what to do.

Find your Authority in the lines below your chart. How do you currently make decisions? How does that method align with your Authority? If it differs, are you open to a new approach?

The focus of this book is to leverage your design to bring your leadership to the next level. If you feel called to dive more deeply into your Type, Strategy, and Authority, I highly recommend Robin Winn's book *Understanding Your Clients Through Human Design: The Breakthrough Technology.*

CENTERS

After Type, Strategy and Authority, you'll want focus next on the Centers in your chart. These are akin to the traditional chakras, though slightly different. Here you'll see there are nine Centers in the shape of triangles, squares or diamonds. Each Center has its own theme and its unique frequency, and each processes information through a particular lens. There are two important aspects to your Centers for you to focus on in your chart: the theme or function of the Center and whether it is Defined (colored in) or Undefined/Open (white). Even with this basic information, you'll be surprised how much you can learn about yourself and others. Let's start with the themes (refer to Chart B below):

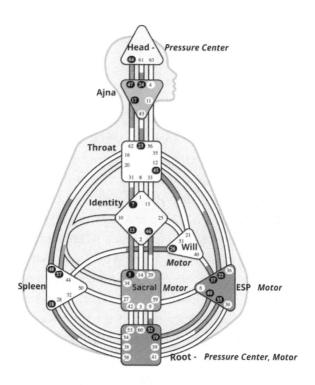

- Head Center – Ideas and inspiration (pressure center)
- Ajna Center – Information processor
- Throat Center – Center for manifestation
- Identity or G Center – Center of lovability and direction in life
- Will Center – Values, ability to commit and to navigate the material world (motor)
- Sacral Center – Sustainable energy (motor)
- Spleen Center – Intuition, fear, immune system health
- Emotional Solar Plexus – Feeling center, creativity (motor)
- Root Center – Adrenalized energy (motor, pressure center)

Side note: here you see that four of the centers are also motors and two of them are also pressure centers. This will be important in later discussions.

DEFINITION AND OPENNESS

When you look at the Centers, you'll notice that they are either Defined (colored in) or Open (white). Defined Centers in your chart provide consistent access to those energies. In fact, you're broadcasting the energy. For example, with a Defined Head Center, you're broadcasting ideas, and with a Defined Emotional Solar Plexus, you're broadcasting feelings and impacting those around you. Where this Center is Open, you're taking in the energy of the people around you and amplifying it. You're receiving their energy or ideas, feelings, and so on. We sometimes refer to the Open Centers as pain points because they're where you can more easily take on other people's beliefs, mistakenly thinking they're yours. We might say, you're not being yourself, and therefore, you're not leading your life. Believing you're someone you're not causes pain, especially when those conditioned patterns are sabotaging your intentions.

If you look at Generators and Manifesting Generators for example, they have Defined Sacral Centers and comprise 70 percent of the population. They have sustainable energy and are designed to actively use their energy to generate. The other three Types, Projectors, Manifestors, and Reflectors, have Open Sacral Centers. They're not designed to have sustainable energy. While they can have more energy than any Generator Type by taking in and amplifying the Defined Sacral energy around them, they can easily burn out. And yet, not knowing their design, they can believe they should be like Generators and Manifesting Generators and act accordingly, pushing beyond their limits. You might begin to see some real-world consequences of living out of alignment with your design.

Look at your chart. Which Centers are Defined? Which are Open? Look at the themes of these Centers. What energy do you have consistent access to? What energies are you taking in and amplifying from the people around you?

There's a wealth of information available when we look at the Definition in our Centers. For an in-depth study of the Centers, I recommend Robin Winn's book *Understanding the Centers in Human Design: The Facilitator's Guide to Transforming Pain into Possibility*. For now, it's enough to know the themes of the Centers, whether they are Open or Defined, and that they point to certain strengths you carry or places where you are vulnerable to conditioning or may give away your Authority. You'll get a deeper understanding of how the Centers function as I share stories of clients weaving in the influence of their different Open and Defined Centers.

We'll also examine these issues a little more closely in Chapter 9.

GATES, CHANNELS, THE PLANETS AND THE I CHING

As we peek into the world of Gates and Channels, the chart takes on another dimensionality and complexity that is inextricably woven together with the placement of the planets at the time of your birth and with the I Ching. If you are not familiar with the I Ching, it's an ancient Chinese Divination tool with sixty-four hexagrams. Like the Centers, each of the sixty-four hexagrams has a set of characteristics associated with it.

Here we get a little technical to create a foundational understanding of how the bodygraph in your chart is created. On either side of the bodygraph there are two columns of information. Each column has a list of planets with numbers next to them. Each number corresponds to one of the sixty-four hexagrams, or what we call Gates. You'll see in the left column that the numbers are in red and the right column's numbers are black.

For example (referring to Chart A in the Appendix), at the top of the Personality column, the number nineteen (in black) is next to the symbol for the Sun. In traditional astrology, the Sun may be in one of twelve zodiac signs; however, it's also in one of sixty-four different hexagrams, so you can begin to appreciate the depth of information available in this system. In this case, Gate 19 is the hexagram for Sensitivity. This person is highly sensitive, longs for intimacy, and has a strong connection to animals. My client Maggie from Chapter 1 (see Chart D in the Appendix) has her Sun in Gate 45, the King/ Queen Gate, so she's here to take leadership and to make sure everyone in her tribe is well cared for. This leadership energy is running all the time whether or not she's stepping into leadership. Others can feel it. That's why she keeps receiving invitations to lead projects or teams.

This list of black numbers on the right is labeled Person-ality because this is who you believe yourself to be – you're conscious of these traits. The red numbers on the left repre-sent the Gates that the planets were in three months before your birth. In Human Design teachings, this is when your soul comes into the body, and you're impacted by these energies. For example, the Unconscious Sun in Appendix A is in Gate 1, Creativity, and this is the most masculine or Yang energy in the system. It's labeled "Design" because this is intrinsic to who you are, and yet you're unconscious about these traits until you discover them in your life journey.

Together, the Conscious and Unconscious Gates make up your bodygraph. As you look further at your bodygraph, you'll see black lines corresponding to the Conscious Gates (the numbers appearing in the right column), and red lines corresponding to the Unconscious Gates (numbers from the left column). When two Gates meet, they become a Channel that has more powerful energy than the individual Gates alone. Think of the difference between a small stream and a large river. The Channels connect the Centers and are the circuitry or flow in the chart.

When you look at Chart A, you'll see Channel 34-10, the Channel of Exploration, is Defined. It links the Identity Center (the yellow diamond) through Gate 10, Self-Love, with the Sacral Center (the pink square) through Gate 34, Power. Both Centers are colored, or Defined, because they have a Channel connecting them. All other Centers in this chart are white, or Open.

PROFILES

Your chart also contains your Profile or learning style. Your Profile adds another layer to understanding your particular style of leadership, as well as appreciating differences in learning styles for the people you're leading. There are twelve Profiles. What is your Profile? If it's a 1/3, then you lead by investigating first and then learn by trial and error. Or perhaps you have a 2/4 Profile. Then you need time alone to hermit before being called out to connect with your network. Maybe you're a 6/3 like Maggie, here to be a role model and to learn by trial and error. There's a wealth of information in those numbers. It's beyond the scope of this basic introduction to give a full explanation. Still, they're important, and I will be speaking at times about the Profiles of clients, so I've included a brief description below.

- 1/3: Investigator/ Martyr: Investigates first and then learns by trial and error

- 1/4: Investigator/ Opportunist: Investigates first and then shares with their network
- 2/4: Hermit/ Investigator: Needs alone time and then is called out to connect with their network
- 2/5: Hermit/ Heretic: Hermits until they call themselves out to lead in crisis with practical solutions
- 3/5: Martyr/ Heretic: Learns by trial and error until needed to provide innovative solutions
- 3/6: Martyr/ Role Model: Learns by trial and error and bringing mature wisdom to the world
- 4/6: Opportunist/ Role Model: Networker, as Role Model, brings wisdom to their network
- 4/1: Opportunist/ Investigator: Investigates and shares with their network, not easily influenced
- 5/1: Heretic/ Investigator: Here to lead in a crisis with practical solutions from investigating
- 5/2: Heretic/ Hermit: Reluctant hermit, universalizes innate gifts and innate talents
- 6/2: Role Model/ Hermit: Wise soul, seeks alone time, unique gifts called out
- 6/3: Role Model/ Martyr: Wise soul, continually learning through trial and error

Note: for a more complete understanding of The Profiles see *Understanding the Profiles: The Facilitator's Guide to Unleashing Potential* by Robin Winn.

DEFINITION

If you look at your chart you will see it says Definition, followed by Single, Small Split, Large Split, Triple Split, or Quadruple Split. Here we're looking at the flow of the Channels in your chart. Does your chart give you a sense of wholeness on your own (because your Defined Centers are connected)? Or does it drive you to connect with others who have specific Gates in their charts (to close a gap to connect all your Defined Centers)? Look at your chart to see which of these types of Definition you carry. This will help you understand why you might operate differently in relationship than others, and what to be aware of in relation to others. As we go through different people's stories you will see how Definition impacts their lives. See the brief descriptions below:

- Single: All Defined Centers in the chart are connected through the Channels. There are no gaps and so there is a continuous flow of energy. You feel a sense of wholeness and independence.
- Small Split: A Gate is needed to bridge the gap or split, so they're electromagnetically drawn to people who have one of the Gates that completes them. They may have a sense that something is missing or something is wrong with themselves.
- Large Split: A Channel or more than one Gate is needed to bridge the split. They're drawn to people who can provide that. They may have a sense that something is missing, or something is wrong with other people.
- Triple Split: Their Defined Centers are in three groupings. They're not looking for someone to complete them. It takes time for them to assimilate information. They're looking to get their flow activated by being in public (for example, in coffee shops). They have a sense of independence.
- Quadruple Split: This rare design has four separate groupings of Defined Centers. They are looking to complete those splits from multiple people; not one person. It's a highly relational design.

INCARNATION CROSS

Lastly your Incarnation Cross is your Life Purpose or theme. It's based on the Gates that your Conscious and Unconscious Sun and Earth are in. This is the most powerful energy in your chart. For example, my Conscious Sun is in Gate 32, Duration, which has the energy of knowing what big dreams to follow. My Conscious Earth is in Gate 42, Endings, which can create order out of chaos and finish things. My Unconscious Sun is in Gate 56, The Storyteller. My Unconscious Earth is in Gate 60, Limitation. When I put them together, I'm here to know which big dreams to follow and to bring them to completion. I do this by telling a new story around limitation. While this isn't new information, having it reflected in my chart supports me in those moments when I'm slipping back into a conditioned idea of who I should be or what I should be doing. My Incarnation Cross brings me back to myself and has become an anchor for me in my life. There are 192 different Incarnation Crosses – too many to list here. I recommend referencing *The Book of Destinies* by Chetan Parkyn and Carola Eastwood, for a full explanation.

Here is an example of my Cross of Limitation from that book:

"Your Life Theme is to provide boundaries and limits so others become aware of the many natural constraints of life. You do this by being realistic about growth potentials, being aware of the possibility of failure, and using the lessons of the past to set expectations for the future. Because you sense the limitations in any given situation and evaluate what realistically can and cannot be achieved, people will always look to you to provide reliable reference points. You are continually seeking balance between maintaining positive and fulfilling growth and succumbing to decline and failure. At times you are likely to be overly cautious, and at other times, you may impulsively push past what

appear to be unnecessary and imposed strictures that hamper a sense of accomplishment. You might take on the role of "survivalist" but, at the same time, be the one who is involved in sustaining growth. Deep within you resides an awareness of the sanctity of life and how it must be honored, preserved, and nurtured at all costs. When confronted by seemingly impossible scenarios, so long as you step back and view everything objectively, you're the one who can endure all challenges and roadblocks until you find a way through... By following your own Type, Strategy and Authority, you will paradoxically be guided to implement changes in stable times and to be still when everyone else is in motion."

Each Incarnation Cross reveals a unique life theme and reflects valuable information for you as a leader. It may reintroduce you to a life path you have forgotten.

This is a simple look at some of the important aspects of the chart, a beginning taste. Hopefully as you begin to look at your chart through the Human Design lens you'll get a new sense of yourself and the possibility of living more closely aligned to your potential. Delving more deeply into your chart, you may experience an unexpected awe and profound gratitude as you recognize your innate brilliance. But we're only at the beginning of our journey. Next we'll go through some important fundamentals – so you can get a feel for aligning with your Type, Strategy, and Authority.

5

ALIGNING WITH YOUR TYPE, STRATEGY, AND AUTHORITY

Working with your Type, Strategy, and Authority allows you to make better decisions, speak in a way you can be heard, impact others, and perhaps have a better understanding of other people's strengths and challenges in their designs. As you come into more alignment with your design, the world will support you in moving toward your goals and your life will become an inspiring journey. See for yourself what happens as you work with your chart.

Let's dive deeper into the five Human Design Types: Generators, Manifesting Generators, Manifestors, Projectors, and Reflectors. Each of these operate differently. Definition in your Centers determines your Type (refer to Chart H below).

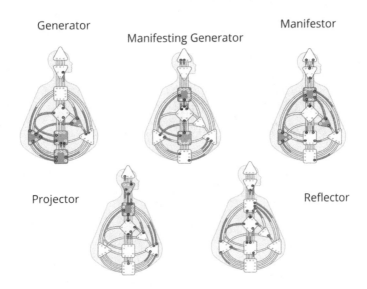

Generator

Manifesting Generator

Manifestor

Projector

Reflector

For example, if you have a Defined Sacral Center, then you're either a Generator or Manifesting Generator. They are both fundamentally Generators. What differentiates Manifesting Generators is that in addition to the Defined Sacral, they have a connection to the Throat Center from one of the four Centers with a motor. This gives them an additional set of gifts.

Following are descriptions of Types and a Strategy for each Type, along with a relevant client or personal story. Listen to their challenges and see if they resonate with you. I'll refer to specific Gates in their charts to illustrate some points. If you're not familiar with these, don't worry about learning those yet. It's most important for you to align with your Type, Strategy, and Authority.

GENERATORS

Generators are highly relational and are here to find their right work, be in response, and co-create with the world around them. They're designed to collaborate rather than manifest on their own. The point of creation, or manifestation, in Human Design is the Throat Center – ideas are manifested or voiced and then impact others who are listening. Without a motor to the Throat Center (refer to Chart B in the appendix for the location of the motors), Generators are not heard unless they're in response to someone else, to a signal in their environment, or to their inner guidance. If they try to initiate rather than respond, their ideas are not heard or their projects don't move forward. However, when they're around someone else who has a motor to the Throat Center, such as a Manifesting Generator or a Manifestor, they have access to this manifestation energy. There are other ways this connection can happen through the Gates. When Generators gain access, they can be heard and impact others. Lacking a motor to the Throat Center is not a weakness; Generators are meant to be in collaboration with others and they are powerful team players.

Generators are gifted with sustainable energy from their Defined Sacral Center, which operates like an internal GPS, giving them guidance by responding to yes/no questions. As long as they have an internal *yes* for what they're doing, then Generators have the ability to work all day long and feel fulfilled. They're here to find their right work and generate or build toward that. However, if they're working on a project that they have an internal *no* for, then their Sacral motor is turned off, their energy drains, and they risk burnout.

Many of my Generator clients are subject to the typical cultural conditioning of overriding themselves, working hard, and doing whatever it takes to get the job done. They don't take time to ask themselves if they have energy for this request, or perhaps they don't dare because they think they can't say *no* anyway. They may find they're in the wrong job and wonder what work will satisfy them. If they ask themselves yes/no questions, they'll naturally find suitable work. Better still someone else can ask them yes/no questions to help them get clear. Finding and mastering their life's work is a natural consequence of consistently following their Sacral responses, and it brings them joy. When they learn to trust this bodily response, they have an invaluable guidance system and more energy for every aspect of their life.

I recently attended a retirement party for Rick, an old friend and work colleague. After dinner, there was an open mic session where people could share their experiences with Rick. I watched as the emcee started speaking and no one listened for the first couple of minutes. Her style was entertaining, and people weren't being rude – they just didn't hear her. As soon as she passed the microphone to the next person, everyone shifted in their seat and turned to listen. This speaker was no better than the previous one, but he likely had a different design.

I also wanted to say something to honor Rick and had made some notes on the drive over to the restaurant. But there was no impulse within me, no signal to step up to the microphone. I waited with curiosity as others spoke about Rick's qualities and named everything I had written in my notes. Finally, when the last person finished, I received a download of what to say, and with that impulse, I picked up the microphone and spoke. Everyone was still and listening attentively as I offered a story that highlighted his openheartedness in a way that no one had yet expressed. People mentioned afterward how moved they were by my words.

What happened with the emcee? I happen to know her Human Design, as well as the design of the first speaker. She has an Open Throat Center, so for her to be heard, someone needs to invite her to speak. Had someone introduced her as the emcee at the beginning, everyone would have listened. The next person who spoke, has a motor to the Throat and gift of being heard when he speaks. That's why the audience paid attention to him. I also have that gift, but it needs to be in response to some signal or request. Consequently, I waited for the inner guidance that prompted me to speak. If that hadn't come, I wouldn't have stepped up to the microphone, because my words wouldn't have been received.

My client Jackie (see Chart C in the Appendix) is a Generator, and she had a tendency to say *yes* to too many things. She has Gate 29, Perseverance, in her Sacral Center, which over-commits and then is unable to back out or delegate. Instead, Jackie perseveres, and her body then takes the hit by coming down with the flu or bronchitis. In her case, it took courage for her to stop this habit and say *no*. First, she needed to build trust in her internal yes/no responses from her Sacral Center. Like most of us, she had been trained to use her head for making decisions, carefully weighing the pros and cons. While the Head Center and Ajna Centers are important for gathering information, organizing, and analyzing it, the actual decision is made by your Inner Authority.

In Jackie's case, you can see her Authority in the lines below her chart, "Inner Authority: Sacral." She has the ability to make decisions in the moment using this yes/no motor response. If the answer isn't clear, she may need more information. She began by asking herself yes/no questions for everyday decisions such as what to eat ("should I eat this apple now?"), what to wear, which task to do next. For more complex decisions, she needed to ask a series of yes/no questions to get clear. For example, she had a deadline on a large project but had a *no* for working on it. In that moment she looked at the various steps of the project to see if there was one with a *yes* response. Otherwise, she could have inquired whether it would help to go for a walk first. There are many possibilities, and it helps to get creative. Learning to ask the right questions is a skill learned with practice.

As she developed a relationship with her Sacral responses, she began to recover energy and became more motivated to continue. Then she took it up a notch by saying *no* to a request for help from a good friend while suggesting other options that might support her. Jackie thought she might be sitting in guilt around it afterward, but instead she felt relief and more energized. When we she was recently asked to take on a project at work and received a clear *no*, she spoke up. Her boss was surprised and a little irritated at first, but her response led to an insightful conversation between them about who would be best suited to do this or whether it was even a priority. Working together they crafted a project plan that became a *yes* for her. They began to collaborate more going forward, which is one of Jackie's strengths.

Jackie clearly wasn't skillful with saying *no* in that conversation with her boss, which is why he was initially taken aback. Fortunately, Jackie's nurturing personality helped her smooth it over. So, we worked together to develop an approach for her that would be more considerate and not so potentially jarring, especially in a work situation:

- Remember that your initial *no* may change as you get more information and be open to that.
- Listen and respect the request.
- Even if you have a *no* response, ask detailed questions about how your boss thinks it could be done more efficiently or if perhaps someone else might be better suited to take this on. You're asking for their viewpoint, not sharing yours here.
- During the conversation, they may decide to suggest an alternative. If not and it's still a *no* for you, then speak to them about it. They may be more open at this point because of your interest and respect.

Likewise, you'll need to stay open and receptive as the conversation unfolds.

Jackie was still struggling with the Generator Strategy to be in response and wanted to revisit that Strategy. With the King/ Queen Gate 45, she is a natural leader, but she doubts herself, because her ideas are not always heard or recognized. She arrived one day at my office particularly upset.

"What happened?" I asked as she plopped down into the chair.

"He did it again. John took credit for my ideas."

I nodded calmly, remembering my experiences with this issue. "Tell me what happened."

She exhaled and said, "I had the perfect idea for reorganizing the Customer Service teams. Last year they tried giving them free doughnuts so they would take fewer breaks and stay at their desks longer. I warned against it at the time saying that we need to fix the underlying problem, not sugarcoat it. Today I brought up a great idea on how to give more support to the teams. I explained that Michelle and Nancy have both shown great leadership potential. I wanted to make them team leads over a smaller pod of employees while they grow into the leadership position. It creates another layer of management but—"

"Okay," I gently interrupted, "I get the picture. How did John take over?" Sometimes I just need to jump in and interrupt Jackie. With her Open Throat Center and the Storyteller Gate 56, she can go on and on. Perhaps it's a reaction to not being heard, but it's like the floodgates open when someone starts actually listening to her.

She understood, "I got lost in my story again. Okay. No one responded. They just nodded and went on with their next agenda item, as if I wasn't even in the room. John did hear me, though, because at the end of the meeting, he said, 'Let's look at giving Michelle and Nancy more responsibilities. They're showing great promise.' What's more, they all agreed, 'Great idea. Send us a proposal.'"

"What did you say to that?"

"I was so shocked I couldn't speak. I'm sure my mouth was hanging open, dumbfounded, as they walked out the door. I was too deflated to confront John in that moment."

"Yes, I can understand your frustration. From your Human Design perspective, do you know what happened here?"

She nodded miserably. "I initiated the idea instead of responding."

"Yes. You had an idea that you were excited about, but rather than wait for someone else to bring up the subject or ask yourself yes/no questions about whether it's appropriate to bring it up then, you threw it out on the table, and it fell on the floor."

"Yes –where John happily pounced on it. I can't reconcile within myself the need to be in response. A good leader is one who initiates, who is seen and heard and impacts others. Besides a great idea should stand on its own merits."

"The idea survived. It would be great for you to feel heard and acknowledged. Patience is required here. Let your ideas incubate until someone asks you a question where these ideas are an appropriate response. You work hard and the employees respect your competence and appreciate your nurturing style. Honor the wisdom you carry by sharing it at the right moment. Leaders use discernment about what to share and when, and sometimes they let others take the credit. Aligning with your Strategy will enhance your natural leadership strengths and give you a sense of satisfaction. Otherwise, with that Open Throat, you'll experience more frustration. Besides – what do you have to lose?"

She brightened and recommitted to aligning more closely with her Type and Strategy.

Jackie had already left one job because her ideas were "stolen." So, she waited. Eventually, someone turned to her at a brainstorming meeting and asked her opinion. When she spoke, everyone listened thoughtfully. After the meeting, her boss complimented her and asked for more clarification about one of her suggestions.

Now Jackie feels more flow in her work, trusts her inner guidance, and waits for the appropriate time to speak. As she consistently worked at it, the other gifts in her chart blossomed and her confidence grew.

If you're a Generator, tune in to your strengths. Take a moment to look at this list and see which ones currently show up in your life: sustainable energy, an inner GPS, a responsive nature, ability to find and pursue your life's work, and your relational nature. You may also be experiencing the Generator challenges. See which of these are troubling you: waiting to respond, lacking a motor to the Throat, trusting your Sacral Center yes/no responses, feeling your energy drain or experiencing burnout. If you're feeling frustrated, this is a clue that you're not aligning with your Generator Type. How would it be to align with your design and watch these challenges resolve or disappear?

Most of the population consists of either Generator or Manifesting Generator Types, so ask people their viewpoints on various issues. If you know they're Generators, ask them yes/no questions so they can tune into their inner GPS and respond appropriately.

MANIFESTING GENERATORS

Manifesting Generators have an extraordinary set of capacities that includes all the gifts of a Generator, plus a motor to their Throat Center. With the ability to be heard and to manifest, they naturally impact people and influence situations. Anyone in their presence gets access to the motor to the Throat, empowering them to be heard and to Manifest. Although Manifesting Generators make great team leaders, they can and often prefer to work on their own. Among their many gifts include the ability to effectively multitask, and as a result, they're generally prolific. As you can imagine, this is a powerfully productive Type - one that our culture admires –and yet it comes with its own set of challenges.

Because of their inherent speed and capacity, Manifesting Generators tend to skip steps, which can be costly, depending on the project. Rather than slowing down, they may need to put strategies in place to compensate, such as informing their team. Their Human Design Strategy is to be in response like the Generator and to inform others before proceeding with their plans. This can be a challenge if the Manifesting Generator is not aware of their impact or if they're worried that someone will challenge their plans. Regardless, their projects will go smoother for them if they take the time to inform others of their plans. This also gives them an opportunity to reflect on how they're impacting the people around them. Just like the Generators, they have the gift of their inner GPS. And with their high capacity for work, they also need to pay particular attention to their Sacral yes/no responses or they risk burnout. When a Manifesting Generator is out of alignment, they become frustrated and angry.

Remember Maggie from Chapter 1? She didn't have an issue being heard; however, she was criticized for not being a team player, and her peers were trying to capitalize on her mistakes. She has several leadership markers in her chart, yet she was passed over for promotions. Let's take a closer look at her Manifesting Generator design (refer to Chart D in the Appendix).

Maggie can easily multitask and has a uniquely large capacity for work with the Channel 44-26, Surrender, linking the Spleen with the Will Center. This Channel is nicknamed the Time Bender Channel because it comes with the huge capacity to produce more in a short period of time than others can even imagine. Therefore, it often seems easier to just do the work than to spend the time and energy delegating. Based on the mix of Channels in her chart, there is further tension around working individually or with a team, so it's important for Maggie to tune into her Sacral yes/no responses for guidance.

While skipping steps was a challenge for her, Maggie began to understand that she was more valuable to the organization operating in the flow and using her speed rather than trying to slow down. She informed her team about this tendency. While it happened less frequently, her peers still made comments. She learned not to give these comments any attention, and they gradually became quieter as well. As a result all that energy she had previously spent trying to stop making mistakes was redirected toward her goals with great results.

You'll notice on Maggie's chart that her Inner Authority is the Emotional Solar Plexus, which means there is an extra step to her decision-making process. She needs to take into account her emotional state before deciding, whereas Jackie, with Sacral Authority, could effectively decide in the moment. People with a Defined Emotional Solar Plexus get clarity over time or from a place of neutrality. Their decision needs to feel good to them, but they can't make effective decisions while they're on an emotional high or at a low point.

This troubled Maggie at first because she is so fast, and her intuition is always available to her with Channel 57-20, The Brainwave. However, she knew something was off with her decision-making so she agreed to track her emotions and come to a place of neutrality before deciding. This step doesn't have to take a lot of time, especially since she has Gate 52,

Stillness. She can tune into that energy for clarity in her deci-sion-making. This is another source of dynamic tension that Maggie needs to navigate in her design – her natural speed vs. the need to slow down in making decisions. She agreed to be patient as she explored this aspect of herself.

Before we worked together, Maggie had started looking for jobs at other companies, believing there wasn't much of a future at her current company. Shortly after this last session on her Inner Authority, she received a job offer and was excited. She wanted to tell them *yes* immediately, but she agreed instead to write down her *yes* response and also her emotional state – "high." When I checked in with her the next morning, she had a *no* response for the job offer. She realized the commute would add another hour to her day and she wanted more time to herself. Again, she wrote down her response and her emotional state – "low." Later that evening she reached clarity. Her final answer was a clear *no* from a neutral state. Maggie realized the pressure she was feeling to respond immediately was from a desire to appear confident and decisive to her potential new employer. She was changing her style to fit what she perceived a new employer wanted. Had she responded with a *yes*, it would have been hard for her to later reject the offer, with her Gate 29, Perseverance. She was grateful for the space to reach clarity. She also realized from this place of stillness that a new job may not be the answer.

If you're a Manifesting Generator, recognize and appreciate the multitude of gifts and capacities you carry, which include the Generator's gifts: sustainable energy, an inner GPS, the ability to find and master your life's work, a responsive and relational nature. In addition, you're gifted with being heard, manifesting, impacting and empowering people, being prolific, multitasking, and acting independently. Take some time to reflect on the abundance you have in this lifetime. Where do these traits show up in your life? Where are you not using these capabilities? Are you grappling with the Manifesting Generator challenges of burnout, doing everything on your own and having to be in response rather than initiate? Where are you skipping steps or not informing people impacted by your decisions? If you're feeling frustrated or angry in some area of your life, you're likely not following your Inner Authority. Learn to trust your Sacral yes/no responses, and if you have a Defined Emotional Solar Plexus, take time to come to place of neutrality before deciding. Are you ready to commit to following your Strategy and Authority and observing what happens? You might find that lots of issues in your life dissolve or resolve as a result of this one shift in behavior.

MANIFESTORS

Manifestors initiate and impact, so their gifts revolve around power and natural leadership. They're here to impact people and situations rather than to be impacted. You can feel this when you're around them because their energy field is streaming toward you, influencing you. They act independently, and with a motor to the Throat, they can speak and be heard. They've been dealt a powerful design, and when you're around them you're empowered too, although you may feel intimidated at first. Only 8 percent of the population has this design. You can imagine what it might be like to try to parent a Manifestor child who is simply not designed to be told what to do. Manifestors with strong parents who tried to rein them in, may have lost connection to their power. When they're reconnected to it, it's such a life-affirming experience. It's like turning on a bright light in a dark room.

Manifestors often experience challenges with relationships. They have an outward streaming aura that can be initially repelling to others. When people ignore that initial impulse to pull away and actually interact with the Manifestor, they usually find them to be approachable or fascinating or worth the effort in some way. Since Manifestors are designed to initiate action and not to receive input from others, this can be challenging in a relationship. They tend to be independent and operate as a lone wolf.

Another challenge for Manifestors is the lack of sustainable energy due to an Open Sacral Center. In the presence of Generators, their Open Centers are receiving and amplifying energy, giving them a huge burst of energy. Manifestors need to monitor themselves to know when enough is enough, or they'll burnout. They're here to impact the direction of life rather than generate with their own energy, and they need rest. Regardless, they have huge capacity. My daughter-in-law is a Manifestor and I watched in awe during her pregnancy, as she handled her normal workload plus all the preparations for the baby, seemingly with ease.

Since Manifestors don't have access to an inner GPS, they need to find their inner guidance system. This can be a challenge for them. Sometimes they just have to try various approaches until one works. One of my (Manifestor) clients, Colleen, says that for her it's like throwing spaghetti against a wall to see what sticks. When we're working together on a project at Flowering Heart Center, I look forward to that moment when she throws ideas against the wall, because her suggestions are always unique and usually effective.

With their Open Sacral Centers, Manifestors do better with open-ended questions. When asked a yes/no question, they automatically go to their Sacral Center where there's no motor, and therefore, no response. Conditioning usually lands in the Open Centers, and so you'll likely get a conditioned response from them from a yes/no question and miss out on their wisdom. By asking them open-ended questions such as,

"What do you think about?" they can respond thoughtfully. Be sure to let them speak uninterrupted, since they can tend to lose their train of thought, and they have much wisdom to share.

The Manifestor Strategy is to Inform and Initiate. It can be difficult for them to inform out of fear that they'll get a negative response. Since Manifestors are not designed to be told what to do, informing is clearly not about asking permission. Rather, it gives others a chance to respond to whatever the impact may be on them. Once the Manifestor realizes that this makes their job easier, they're more inclined to follow this Strategy.

One of my Manifestor clients, Sarah, was silenced as a child because she was "wild and bossy," and they didn't know how to handle her (see Chart E in the Appendix). She said, "My dad was tough on me and thought he was doing me favor by teaching me to obey authority." Fortunately, she came into her power as a young adult when she met her husband and he saw her for who she truly was. This was her first experience of being seen, and over time, she stepped back into her power.

She came to me because she had wisdom to share and wanted better relationships with others so she could have deep conversations with them. She could see how her presence and her speaking sometimes turned people off.

As we looked at her chart, it was clear that she has the gift of expressing breakthrough insights in a way that can be understood with Channel 43-23, Structuring. If she speaks in the wrong timing, she may be seen as a freak and experience rejection. If spoken at the right time, people will seek her out for her wisdom and clarity. Additionally, she has Gate 30, Passion, so her speaking would sometimes come across too strongly. Finally, as a Manifestor, people would unconsciously be repelled at first, until they actually spoke with her.

Sarah worked first on relationship with her Inner Authority, the Emotional Solar Plexus, learning to come to a place of neutrality within herself before deciding. Then she could clearly hear the still small voice of her inner guidance. This practice of tuning in supported her to speak her breakthrough ideas in the right time.

Sarah was working through some childhood trauma that led her to be overly concerned about pushing others away before getting to speak with them. We were able to soften that initial impact on others by using a visualization technique. First, she made sure she was in her heart, accessing Gate 10, Self-Love. Then she practiced placing her awareness on the other person, visualizing them receiving what they most desired. She was surprised how this shifted the energy so significantly that strangers were often well-disposed toward her. As she became more skilled in following her Inner Authority, people sought out her out opinions more, and Sarah was able to channel her passion into helping them make breakthroughs.

Are you a Manifestor? How would you describe your relationship to your power? How can you better align with your Strategy to inform before acting? Take a moment to appreciate the powerful gifts you embody and contemplate where they show up in your life: natural leadership, initiating, impacting others, speaking and being heard, acting independently.

Some of those gifts can also be a challenge, such as impacting people by your presence, acting independently in relationships, and having natural power and capacity when others don't. How do you handle the lack of sustained energy? What happens when you don't follow your Strategy to Inform and then Initiate? How is your relationship to your inner guidance? How do you access it? Look at how you're currently dealing with any of these challenges. When you're experiencing anger in your life, you're likely disconnected from your Type, Strategy, and Authority. How can you more closely align with your Manifestor self and fully claim your power?

PROJECTORS

Projectors are the wise guides of humanity and comprise about 21 percent of the population. Like Manifestors they have an Open Sacral Center and impact the room with their presence. However, Projectors impact in a way that is unseen – like an orchid in the room. The orchid brings an uplifting presence but it's subtle until you see it. Then you appreciate its beauty.

Projectors have no motor to the Throat where they could be seen and heard. They're lacking any consistent access to generating or manifesting energy, and yet they're the leaders of the future. They're here to direct the other energy Types and are like hidden jewels waiting to be discovered. When they're recognized and invited to share, their wisdom impacts powerfully. Projectors have a strategic maturity where they can see what needs to be done and how to use people's talents in the best way. They can increase the effectiveness and productivity of Generators, Manifesting Generators, and Manifestors. Rather than telling others what to do, they guide by asking questions.

Projectors are magnetic and draw people to themselves when they're involved in projects they love or being happily quiet, in a location that feels good to them. This works well with their challenging Strategy to "Wait for Recognition and Invitation." Without that recognition or invitation, they are powerless and remain hidden. Anything they say is not received. Their job is to wait for the right invitation. Waiting can be difficult, and they might want to jump at the first invitation, but they must tune in to their Inner Authority to see if it's a match. If so, the one who invited them receives a wise and powerful ally, and the Projector feels free to offer their many gifts. My teacher, Robin illustrates how this Projector Strategy works in a vivid way in her book, *Understanding Your Clients Through Human Design: The Breakthrough Technology*. She relates the story of a Projector client who was invited to be on a prestigious board that met monthly in New York. This woman prepared carefully for the board meetings, but whenever she tried to offer her viewpoint, she couldn't get a word in edgewise. No one asked her opinion. Her coach suggested she continue to show up prepared each month, and not say anything until asked. She also suggested that this woman enjoy her all-expense paid trips to New York. It took several months for anyone to ask her a question in those board meetings. As soon as someone did, she shared her ideas in great detail and the room went silent. Everyone was shocked by her level of understanding and the depth of her offering. She was then considered an integral part of all subsequent meetings. Can you feel the power of this Strategy? In this case, the Projector received knowledge of her design and was able to reframe her business trips to pleasurable excursions until she was called on for her expertise. Many Projectors out there are navigating blindly, not understanding why they're not seen or appreciated – and the rest of us are missing their valuable contributions.

One of my Projector clients, Patty, joined my Lead by Design training because she was feeling burned out and somewhat bitter (see Chart F in the Appendix). She was conditioned from a young age to work hard, and because she is blessed with the Time Bender Channel 44-26, she has capacity to complete large quantities of work in a short period of time. With her Defined Will Center, she can also be counted on to follow through on her commitments. Maybe with what you've learned so far, you can appreciate how she has been overriding herself by acting like a Generator. No wonder she is burned out! It can be a struggle for Projectors to monitor their energy and not overdo things. For Patty, this issue is magnified.

Looking at her chart, you might notice she also has a Defined Throat Center. Of course, since there is no motor connected, she's lacking the ability to manifest and impact. While she does have consistent access to her voice and a sense of assuredness, others can't hear her unless she is recognized or invited to speak. With the Channel 11-56, Curiosity, composed of the Gate 11, Ideas, and Gate 56, Storyteller, Patty would express her ideas in stories to anyone who would listen, without waiting for an invitation. Of course, people didn't respond well, and she felt a profound sense of rejection, wondering if her stories had any value. She instinctively knew that they did, but she was perplexed and needed guidance.

First, she had to drop the belief that her value was tied to producing and begin to embody her design, which impacts simply by her presence. Next, Patty needed to follow her Strategy of "Wait for Recognition and Invitation." She was reluctant to do this since her new healing business was ready to launch, and she felt the need to put herself out there. However, since her energy was low from overextending herself, she agreed to follow her Strategy. While waiting for the right initiation, she focused on doing what she loved. Patty found contentment while writing her story and singing in her cozy home. As her energy returned, she found herself fully enjoying this experience.

Within three weeks, a woman who owned an alternative healing company contacted her. She had found some old posts online where Patty recounted her heroic life journey. This woman invited Patty to offer her energy work at their new center. I reminded Patty to check with her Inner Authority to make sure this was the right invitation for her. On her chart, you can see that her Inner Authority is Splenic. This means she tunes in to her intuitive knowing in the Spleen Center for guidance. Patty received the guidance to go forward, and she reported back that she felt "really seen for the first time," by someone other than her husband.

Sometimes it takes longer for a Projector to get the invitation. Eileen came to me frustrated because she was a performance artist and wanted to share her new work with the world. She commented that living in the Chicago suburbs was not her idea, but at least her husband had a short commute to work. When I asked where she preferred to live, she said she couldn't even consider that for a few years with her husband's job situation.

I said, "Let's wave a magic wand. Where would you choose if you could?"

She somewhat reluctantly said, "New York."

I encouraged her to arrange weekend trips there a few times a year. It's not that far from Chicago, and it would put her in an environment where she was more likely to receive the right invitations. It took over a year for that invitation to come, but it would never have arrived at her doorstep in the suburbs of Chicago.

You may remember that my grandson Jack from Chapter 2 is a Projector. His parents will need to support him by observing the ways in which he interacts with healthy energies early on. With the openness in his chart, Jack is taking in and amplifying the energies of others and needs to be aware of which energies are good for him to be around. He also needs to learn when he is recognized and what a correct invitation feels like. In Jack's case it may be challenging for him to wait to speak because he has Channel 43-23, Structuring and Gate 4, Answers in his Conscious Sun. He'll likely want to blurt out his breakthrough insights on impulse. His parents can invite and recognize him, giving him plenty of opportunities to speak his opinions and potentially way-out-there ideas. In this way he can feel the powerful being that he is. His training needs to include learning to wait for recognition and invitation so his breakthrough solutions can be received by others. These conversational and energetic skills will put him on a path to being a successful adult.

Are you a Projector? What do you notice about the magnetic quality that you carry? How can you focus more on what you love doing? Take a look at your environment at home and work to see if it feels good to you. What invitations have you received? Take some time to reflect on this Strategy of "Wait to Be Recognized and Invited." How can you incorporate that into your life or deepen your commitment to it? How do you manage your energy level? Be sure to allow yourself time to rest and recover from the Generator energy that you take in from other people around you. Take some alone time before you sleep at night.

What is your Inner Authority? Check your chart. It may be your Emotional Solar Plexus, Splenic or another type of Authority. The other types of Inner Authority are sometimes called "No Authority." In these cases, your guidance comes from listening to yourself speak to a neutral listener. Let people know to ask you open-ended questions so your wisdom can flow through.

If you're feeling bitter about life, that's an indication that you are out of alignment with your Type, Strategy, and Authority. Make the commitment to follow it and see what happens. Appreciate the wisdom you carry. Others will recognize it and invite your guidance. The world needs you.

If you know any Projectors, invite them to speak and listen to what they have to say.

REFLECTORS

Only 1 percent of the population are Reflectors, which is where all nine Centers are Open or undefined. Each of these Centers is taking in information from other people and the environment and amplifying it. This is a fluid structure that allows Reflectors to experience everything and consequently merge with the world around them. They're here to awaken and experience Oneness. As a result they have mirrorlike quality in the presence of others. When you're seeing a Reflector, you're looking into the mirror and seeing yourself. In this way, they also reflect the health of the communities they live in. This means you're not seeing the Reflector, and they may feel invisible.

It can be challenging for a Reflector to discover who they are, or to ground themselves or make decisions. Their openness means they can easily lose themselves in other people' ideas, feelings, fears, values, and energy. It's important for them to live in a space that feels good to them, in a community that feels welcoming to them. Because they're constantly taking in all of this information, they need plenty of rest and time alone.

When it comes to decision-making, the founder of Human Design, Ra, says they need a whole lunar month to decide. The Reflectors I've encountered don't feel they need that much time. But they do need a significant amount of time to integrate the information that is flowing through them and come to clarity. If they're considering a big decision, perhaps waiting a month would be the best approach.

Barbara walked into my life at the beginning of my spiritual teaching journey. I'd been leading organizations in the corporate world for twenty years, but I had only been exploring the spiritual world for seven years and was still unlearning so much. She joined my weekly Byron Katie groups and made an impact right away. She was full of anger and highly reactive. She thought other people, especially her family, were to blame for her circumstances. The Byron Katie questions were hard for her, but she stuck with them. I was impressed with her determination. Over the next twelve years, she journeyed with me to Oneness University in India, attended our weekly blessings circles and also worked with me privately.

Something about her intrigued me. It took a long time for her to stop engaging in constant drama, and so my interactions with her could be quite rough. Yet I listened. When she gave me feedback about my teaching style or the community or programs, I always took note. She was observant, gave good advice and always had the welfare of the whole community in mind. She also had a broader perspective and interesting viewpoints about what was happening in the world. She worried about world events as if she could and somehow needed to do something about them.

Naturally, when I started my Human Design journey, I offered her a session. When I pulled up her chart, I stared in shock. Suddenly it all made sense. She was a Reflector (see Chart G in the Appendix). No wonder she had trouble navigating life. She was walking in life completely open trying to get a handle on who she was, what she valued, what she was feeling, and wondering why she didn't she have energy. She took on other people's beliefs simply to find some solid ground. Finally, she was waking up and wanting more freedom in her life. Barbara began to consistently put in the effort to release sabotaging beliefs, to stop engaging in drama and to connect with her inner guidance. I consider her presence in our community a treasure.

I realize now that the "something special" I felt around her was partly my reflection. Reflectors' mirroring quality means that when you're with them you see yourself – including parts you don't want to see. I had to use my Byron Katie tools often in the beginning of our relationship, to release my judgments. I would see things about myself, or she would give me feedback that required more work on my part to own and shift. As I grew, I appreciated that mirror even more. As she grew, the mirror became clearer and more powerful.

Based on the Gates in her chart, Barbara is here to disseminate knowledge to those who are ready to learn from her. Others may be put off by it at times, but I value her ability to offer practical solutions that make life better.

Since I've discovered Barbara is a Reflector, I have been more conscious about asking her opinions on the programs we're offering or how they're received. Reflectors mirror the health of the community that they are involved with, and I am grateful for this support.

Are you a Reflector? How have you navigated life with your Open Centers? Contemplate your gifts and how they show up for you: being a clear mirror, fluidity, ability to be one with nature and to connect with all things?

Reflect on the challenges you've experienced with your fluidity and potential lack of bearings. How do you compensate for this openness? Tune in to see if you're in the right environment and communities. If not, how can you shift those? How do you currently make decisions? Be sure to arrange your schedule to get plenty of rest. How does this mirrorlike quality show up in your life?

Reflectors can experience a profound sense of disappointment at times because they see what is possible in situations and people. Disappointment is a signal that you're not aligning with your Type, Strategy, and Authority. It's also somewhat inherent in your design. With so much openness, it may be hard to remember or to understand that others are not as fluid or as able to connect deeply with people and the world around them. If you know someone who is a Reflector, ask them open-ended questions and be prepared to see yourself in their answers. Honor their ability to merge with the world around them, their worldview, and their wisdom, which comes – in my experience – without judgment.

SUMMARY

The five Human Design Types are like pieces of a puzzle that fit together. All of them have their part to play and are vitally important to a well-functioning company or society. In a perfect world, Manifestors would be free to initiate processes. Generators and Manifesting Generators would align to their natural power as creative builders. Projectors, with their capacity to see the big picture, recognize the gifts and talents of others and bring people together, would effectively guide the work. However, they would need an invitation from the other energy Types to lead. Reflectors would tell us how we are doing, while the other Types would be open to receive this assessment. All Types have great capacity for leadership – there is no hierarchy among them. When you're aligning with your Type, Strategy, and Authority, you'll feel the joy of living your Type.

What have you learned about yourself? Do you have a better sense of how aligning with your design can help you make better decisions, communicate effectively, and impact others? Perhaps you also have a sense of the other layers you can explore as you move deeper into Human Design, including the Centers, Channels, and Gates. Take a moment and look at your bodygraph again. Take three slow deep breaths as you do this. Maybe you can even catch a glimmer of the magnificence of your design.

6

ALIGNING WITH THE WORLD DESIGN

N ow that you've aligned with your Human Design, you'll be more effective if you're also aligned with what I call the World Design. Your current reality, what is happening in the present moment, is defined or fixed. However, the future reality is open and fluid. Furthermore, it's operating in response to you. You're constantly sending signals either consciously or unconsciously, and the future is unfolding accordingly.

When you're unconscious, or operating on automatic, you're reacting to what is happening around you and sending signals to the future reality for more of what you're resisting. It responds, although usually with a delay. In this state, you've lost control of your attention and the conditioning in your Open Centers is sending the signals, creating your reality. When you're awake or in control of your attention, you can consciously take action steps toward your goals, and the world will respond by supporting you.

The world is a giant mirror, reflecting back what you present to it. You're the creator of your reality, and you can proceed on automatic or with awareness. Let's develop some skills so your Human Design can work in concert with the World Design to create the reality you prefer.

Let's see how Maggie responds to this concept and learns to create what she prefers.

Maggie had been aligning more closely with her design as a Manifesting Generator by being in response, listening to her Sacral yes/no answers and tracking her emotional wave for clarity. She was already seeing the results of making better decisions. My plan was to orient her to the nature of the outer world so that her journey would be smoother.

First, she needed to understand how the world is a giant reflection field. This is a concept familiar to both traditional religions and new age spirituality. According to the Bible, "You reap what you sow only many times over." According to *A Course in Miracles*, "Whatever is lacking in relationship is what you're not giving." Then there is the new age version, "as above so below." These words of wisdom are pointing to the world mirror. What you present to it is what you receive.

"Yes, I know that," Maggie replied when I rattled off those quotes. She had heard these sayings so often over the years that they'd lost their meaning.

I needed to slow her down, so she could grasp the enormity of this idea. "Let me bring it home to you. Come stand in front of this mirror. Ask for something."

She walked over to the mirror on the wall. "Okay. I want a raise so I can afford a vacation in Italy."

I suppressed a smile, "What do you notice?"

"What?"

"Say it again and watch what is happening with your image in the mirror."

"I want a raise so I can afford a vacation in Italy."

"Can you tell me what you noticed?"

"The image is asking me for a raise so it can go on vacation."

"Exactly."

"So?" Maggie was perplexed.

"Whatever you present to the mirror is what you receive.

You have presented wanting.

You receive more wanting.

You then experience more wanting."

"All right" Maggie was still mystified. "What do I do? Give the image a vacation?"

"Close. Let's try another example first," I said spotting a vase of flowers on my desk. I picked up the red rose and walked back to Maggie.

"Do you like to receive flowers from people?"

"Of course. Who wouldn't?"

"Okay, take this flower and present it to the mirror. Can you tell me what you notice now?"

"The image is giving me a flower."

"Yes."

"Okay, but how do I give the image a vacation or a raise? For that matter, do I really need to give it anything?"

"What you offer is what you receive, with a delay. You could offer money to someone who needs it. Maybe you can be so bold as to pay for a hotel for someone who needs a vacation."

"Wait. I need money to go on vacation and the only way to receive it is to spend money for someone else to take one?" Maggie stood with her arms crossed facing me defiantly.

"It's not the only way, but this is powerful."

I remember being at Oneness University in India where Sri Bhagavan told a man who was going blind to pay for the eye surgeries of everyone in his hospital that day. He knew the man had money and the man trusted Sri Bhagavan. He did as he was told and paid for five eye surgeries. His sight started to return and eventually came fully back to him. I've never forgotten that story.

Maggie stirred. "I'm not convinced, but I'm still listening. Keep talking."

"Now, you have your inner GPS. Ask yourself yes/no questions to find out what to give and to whom. See what answers you get. Maybe you'll receive an answer that you can act on now."

I continued to explain that there is one thing she needed to understand about this world mirror. What you present is what you receive; however, it takes time to materialize. Matter takes time to form. Because of the delay, people don't realize the extent to which the world is a reflection field. Many teachings point to this phenomenon. The concept couldn't be clearer, but standing in front of a real mirror drives the point home.

Now this mirror responds to more than your actions. It responds to your thoughts and words. In fact, the most powerful thoughts are ones attached to strong emotions. This is where you get into trouble. Suppose you decide to pay for that hotel room for a friend who is exhausted from taking care of a sick family member. While you're making the reservation you suddenly feel resentful: "I can't believe I'm spending this on someone else when I'm the one who is aching to get away." The mirror is reflecting your resentment back to you with more reasons to be resentful. You take the bait, your resentment intensifies, and you encounter more roadblocks. While your action of giving was helpful, it was co-opted by the resentful thoughts, and you never receive the benefits of that gift.

"Is this making sense?"

Maggie looked troubled. "What do I do? I can't stop my feelings."

"Nor should you. That will intensify the resentment. Allow the feeling but don't focus on it. Keep your attention on the fact that you want to give this to your friend. Now this thought may return again. If it does the first defense is humor.

Imagine a cartoonish picture in your head of the witch that you are. Use your creativity. If it keeps returning, use the Surfacing Beliefs Process" (found in Appendix B).

Maggie nodded, still skeptical. "I'll start with some smaller desires and see how that goes."

"Perfect. Enjoy the exploration."

The following week she returned, looking worried. Suddenly the mirror concept was becoming burdensome.

Maggie had lots of questions. "How do I watch all of my thoughts? Do you know they're mostly negative? Are all those thoughts ruining my life?"

"First, thoughts attached to emotions are the more powerful ones. Those are the ones to watch. Secondly, celebrate the fact that you're becoming more aware. There are rogue programs running in your unconscious sabotaging your success and now you're finally starting to see them. Awareness is the first step and the most important one. Without it you might as well not leave your house."

"But why am I so negative?"

"Those are not your thoughts. In India, they refer to the thoughtsphere – the space in which thoughts arise and travel. You're presented with hundreds if not thousands of thoughts in any given microsecond. You choose which thought to latch onto. Since we live in a duality, every thought has a positive and negative side to it. You can latch on to a positive thought and turn it negative or choose the positive side of the negative thought. You can choose not to latch on to any thoughts, but this takes dedicated practice. Eventually they let go of you.

For example, you might have the thought: "Hurray! We get ice cream for dessert. Oh, no, this will fatten my hips."

Once you choose the negative side of a thought, you set off a chain reaction of chemicals in your system causing you to feel worse. You can actually see the impact by looking in the mirror. Your facial expressions and body posture change depending on whether you align with the negative or positive side of the thought."

Maggie looked worried, "How does anyone ever leave their front door and venture out then?"

"We're asleep to the fact that in every moment we create our world, our experience of reality is shaped moment to moment. Instead, people blame others or the weather or their financial condition, thinking their happiness lies outside themselves. So, they're free to venture out, unaware of the consequences of their thoughts, words, and actions. The magic of creating our reality happens within and the mirror is a great tool to help us wake up and see more clearly what we're creating."

"Show me."

"Okay. Stand in front of the mirror again."

MIRROR EXERCISE

Now notice where your attention goes first.

Maggie looked carefully at herself. "Oh, I didn't realize I have a whole new set of freckles there. I was out in the sun yesterday."

"Do you know what just happened here?"

"I noticed my freckles."

"Yes, your attention went to what's wrong with your image."

"How did you know I don't like freckles?" Maggie challenged.

"By your tone of voice and your wrinkled-up face," I replied evenly.

"So, the mirror will reflect back to me more reasons to wrinkle my face."

I smiled, "Yes. Now, you took the negative side of that

thought about freckles and then embellished the story by
attaching a reason, 'I was out in the sun.'"

"So?"

"You're believing your thought that you don't like freckles
or that they don't enhance your beauty. Then you're making it
stronger by finding evidence."

"Well, they don't enhance my beauty."

"And the mirror will agree with you, and so it is."

I moved on to the next step: "Now when you look in the
mirror, ignore that first impulse to find what's wrong. Instead,
look for attributes you like in yourself."

"Let me see. I'm tall and have a great tan and... " Maggie
frowned, "these pants look too tight on me."

"That started out great. See how quickly the mind moves
to the negative? It's a well-worn groove in your consciousness
so this will take practice."

I moved on to the last step in this exercise, "Let's take this
a step further. Close your eyes. Smile. Keep smiling. Now hold
the smile as you open your eyes and find what is right and
beautiful about you."

"I have a soft welcoming presence."

"Great. Was that your first thought or did you have to
discard a negative one first?"

"No, that was my first thought."

"Perfect. The world will reflect back to you that there is
nothing wrong with you. You're perfect as you are and have a
welcoming presence."

I added as Maggie was turning to leave, "If you keep
getting negative first thoughts, keep practicing this until your
first impulse is what is right with you."

After Maggie left, I thought about the road ahead of her –
how more awareness brings more insights into the parts of
ourselves we love to hide. The payoff is freedom, but the

initial stage of seeing the negativity and the self-centered behavior can be a bit daunting.

She continued to work at it, by stopping at intervals during the day, noticing her reality, observing where her attention was focused, and redirecting as needed. She began to enjoy life more, treating the practices like a game with life.

I continue to work with these concepts on a daily basis. Recently I completed a yearlong coaching program with Marianne Williamson. I heard the phrase over and over, "Whatever is lacking in relationship is what you're not giving." I realized I was not acknowledging my partner, Frank, for all that he did for me. He went through a period of feeling down and frustrated. I started bringing more awareness to him and acknowledging what he said and complimenting him more. I would respond, "You're right" or "I would never have thought of it that way. Brilliant." I watched him lighten up more and more until his old self was back. I wanted more lightness in our relationship, and I received it by giving him what he seemed to want – attention and acknowledgment. In fact, everyone desires to feel significant, so you can uplift your relationships in this way.

Your intuition will tell you what to offer the other person in order to deepen your connection. Spirit is always happy to offer input on questions that benefit other people. As a byproduct, you receive the benefit too.

What a glorious world this is.

I look at the mirror, and it reflects glory back to me.

7

LEADING BY SETTING YOUR DIRECTION

Now that you're more aligned with your Human Design and have some experience with the World Design, your next task is to choose your destination. If you don't know where you're headed then someone else is leading. You might think that your work goals give you direction – and they do. However, the company in which you work – even if it's yours – is leading you. The beauty of setting a goal for your life is that it's uniquely yours and is inspiring, especially when it's your soul's goal for you. You can start by reading about your Incarnation Cross from your Human Design chart. This will give you an overall life theme. Then tap into your higher self through the G Center for your specific life purpose or goal.

When you come into a place of stillness and tune in to the G Center, you can connect with the Divine spark that is your essence. If you ask, you'll receive an impression of your soul's intention. Accept whatever you receive and begin to express it in words. Craft intentions that succinctly capture the goal and keep tuning in until you land on one that feels right. Then you can align your work goals to your overall intention and feel more motivated. If you reach a point where the work goals diverge from your life goals, it may be time to consider a change in employment or to renegotiate your responsibilities at work.

Let's start this exploration at the beginning step. In order to move in the direction of your destination, you need to know your starting point. How are you currently leading your life? (If you're a Generator or Manifesting Generator, answer this question, Do you know how you're currently leading your life?) The world mirror has been reflecting this back to you. Let's look at what Maggie had discovered about her leadership experience.

Maggie was back in my office feeling excited about her new insights.

My questions threw her a curve ball. "Now I know you're anxious to get on with your life. You've aligned with your design and are working with the world mirror, but where are you going? And do you really know your starting point?"

She seemed startled. "Of course, I know my starting point. I'm standing right here."

I nodded, agreeing, "Yes. From here, look around at your current reality. You've started developing more awareness in the last couple of weeks. What have you learned in that process?"

"I'm seeing how many of my motivations are about 'What's in it for me?' it's a little embarrassing, and I have no idea where that came from. I realize that the mirror will give me more of that so I'm working with my humor. It keeps cropping up though. As a leader, this is not a great platform to stand on."

"Excellent! Great awareness. We can work with that. This is a common stance coming from your survival instincts. The more you try to sweep it away and appear unselfish to other people, the more your emotions will betray you. The mirror will reflect back selfishness. You have to accept this part of your nature."

"If I accept it then won't I get more of it?"

"Not exactly. By acceptance, I mean acknowledge its right to exist. It's a human feeling that everyone experiences. Rather than indulging in it, accept the selfishness and then ignore it and shift your focus elsewhere. Acceptance releases the energy behind it rendering it powerless before the world mirror. The more you accept it the more humorous and harmless it becomes. Conversely, the more you try to avoid it, the more you empower it. And if your destination includes embodying leadership without selfishness, you need to disempower it right now. Anything you're avoiding in your current reality sticks to you like glue and comes with you to your new destination."

"Wow. Okay. Accept but don't focus on it. I believe I can do that and hope the humor comes naturally at some point."

"Trust me. Your perspective will shift and you'll be amused by the thoughts and the mind's antics. Now, let's continue working on your leadership. Can you tell me what your current story of leadership is?"

"What do you mean, 'story?'"

"Do you know how you would describe yourself as a leader right now?"

"I try to be true to my vision and work hard toward the goal. I try to be a good example for others and inspire them to align behind a common vision."

"I appreciate your desire to be that. Let's look at what is true right now in your current reality. What story does that tell? For example, Can you tell me what your team would say about your leadership? Your boss? Your peers?"

"Hmm. My team would say I have high expectations and that they don't feel fully acknowledged. My boss might say I need to communicate more with my peers, to be more of a

team player. My peers? They would say that I'm so busy with
my work, that they never see me. They would like more interaction. They see me as competitive."

"Great. Now look at your experience in your work life and
what you just communicated to me. Can you tell me your
current story of leadership at work?"

"I'm hardworking, focused on the goal, to the exclusion of
others at times. I set a high bar for others to meet and could
use more compassion because others...," Maggie thought for a
moment. "Others are not designed like me. I'm starting to
realize that not everyone has my capacity or my energy level. I
need to recognize and work with each person's strengths."

"Excellent. You're awareness is really growing. Your
current story is what you're experiencing as your reality. The
beliefs you hold about your leadership are being reflected to
you and reinforcing those beliefs. See how the mirror works?"

"I believe so."

"This is the beauty and majesty of this world. Any set of
rules you adopt, the mirror says, 'So be it.' They become your
experience. When you truly realize this, you can take ownership and adopt rules that support where you want to go. Isn't
this amazing?"

"Why hasn't that worked for me before?"

"It has. Your current reality is unfolding from the beliefs
you currently hold, but many of those beliefs are unconscious.
Some of them are other people's ideas that have landed in
your Open Head Center, and you believe they're yours. You've
been operating with them so long that you can't see them. It's
like a dirty windshield: only when you clean it, do you realize
just how dirty it was. Beliefs like 'I'm not loveable' or 'I don't
deserve this' can have a huge impact on you over time. They
impact your relationships, success, and health. They're
programs running in the subconscious, but once you see them
you can choose not to align with them. Most of our issues in

life go back to beliefs we took on at an early age. The mirror has been reinforcing them all this time and they've become transparent to you. One way to find the sabotaging beliefs you have running is to look closely and objectively at your current reality. Are you ready for this?"

"Yes."

"Are you willing to see the things that you've been hiding from yourself?"

"Yes, perhaps."

"I love your honesty. Let's explore. Come from a place of curiosity and nonjudgment. You can pretend you're looking at someone else's life if that helps you be more objective. You need to see and acknowledge everything. That doesn't mean condoning it but, rather, acknowledging its right to exist. Let's begin."

CURRENT REALITY CONTEMPLATION

Close your eyes
Take two slow deep breaths
Now tune in for a moment to the leader you want to be.
Don't worry about getting it perfect. You've already mentioned about living true to your vision and inspiring others to work toward a shared goal. Feel free to edit or embellish that one.
Now, take a deep breath in and let that go.
Relax the body on the out breath.
Inhale again and hold at the top of the inhale.
Exhale all the air out.
Draw the naval back to the spine.
Hold the air out.
Inhale deeply and hold.
Gently release. Take long slow breaths.
Bring your attention to your heart.

Connect with your guidance, with Source.

Ask for support to see what you need to see to take your leadership to the next level.

Slow deep breaths.

Now imagine you're an alien, living on a planet somewhere out in the galaxy.

You're meeting with your supervisor.

He is giving you an assignment – to look at a typical day in the life of a human on Earth.

You're going to Earth to observe, gather data, and bring it back to share with others who have a similar assignment.

You're so excited because you've always wanted to visit this planet.

You're curious by nature.

It's such a beautiful planet.

You step into your vehicle, and it materializes instantly in the atmosphere of Earth.

No one notices you.

You are also invisible.

Your alien self slows down and steers the craft to your home, where you live.

Your alien self has landed in your Earth self's yard.

She is getting out of the vehicle and looking around curiously at the landscape, the people, the buildings, the dogs, the trees.

She pauses at your front door. What will she find?

She opens the door cautiously and looks inside.

No one can see her, but still she wants to be respectful.

She looks around the room observing.

Is anyone home?

What does the room look like?

Are kids running around?

Is the TV on? What are they watching?

She walks slowly through, looking into each room.

In the kitchen – what are people eating?

Is there food on the stove or to-go containers from a restaurant?

What's in your refrigerator? Your cabinets?

There is so much information to take in, but this alien can handle it.

She's looking under carpets.

Wow, nothing escapes her.

She also senses energy really well.

She can tell if there's tension between family members or harmony.

She's there for a couple of days observing interactions over meals, and during TV shows.

She joins family members running errands.

She periodically senses the energies in each room.

Are these people enjoying life?

Are they overwhelmed, overworked, or low on energy?

She listens in on conversations.

Are people protective and shut down?

Is someone wanting attention?

Are they respectful of each other or do they take each other for granted?

As she checks the home office, she senses your relationship to your computer and the people you call for business.

She can tell how productive you are and how much stress is there.

Nothing is hidden from the alien.

It's all out in the open.

She also visits your office building.

She's watching the employees interacting.

She tunes in to what your boss thinks of you and what your team thinks about you.

She senses areas of tension and places where people abuse power.

It's amazing how much the alien can absorb.

Now she's following the kids to school, soccer games, friends' houses.

If they're grown up and gone, she goes to their homes and observes their families.

She gets a sense of the harmony or disharmony in their space.

She checks in with your pets. They have conversations.

The cat refuses to talk with her, but she tunes in to the cat's thoughts anyway.

She tunes in now to see if there is any area missing.
She checks out the health club.
How busy human life is!
It's just an observation. No judgment.
She has nothing to compare it to.
The interactions between people could be passionate or angry.
She doesn't have a reference point for it.
She is simply intrigued and amazed at the breadth of experiences.
She's busy taking in information and sorting through it.
She completes her investigation and steps back in the vehicle.
The alien returns to her home world grateful for this fantastic adventure.
She's excited to share.
She meets her boss right away in his conference space.
The boss asks, What did you learn?
What are humans like?
Now listen as the alien reports back to her supervisor what she has observed,
Notice what's most important in her mind.
She speaks without judgment.
It's a scientific readout.
Listen to your report to your supervisor without judgement, as if it were about someone else.
Have the same curiosity as the aliens.

After listening, make notes in a journal, especially of the issues that have been hidden.

What haven't you wanted to see?

Observe it without judgment. Acknowledge its right to exist; then let it go.

If you have trouble releasing, then refer to Appendix C for "Running the Energy behind the Charge Process."

CHOOSING A NEW REALITY

Now that you have a handle on your starting point, your current reality, it's time to pick a destination or new reality. Without a clear direction and destination, you allow yourself to be blown about by the winds of life or you allow yourself to be swept into other people's agendas. Your goal is your North Star. Take hold of the wheel, choose your direction, and steer.

Remember that this goal is for your whole life (not just for work). That may sound a little grand, and your mind may tell you to make it simple and small; we're not interested in what goal your mind would set. What goal is in your heart? What is your soul's goal for you? If you're not clear, set a goal for self-development or self-acceptance and in that journey your true goal will arise.

Maggie was reflecting on her experience of the current reality.

"I don't want to live small. I have capacity and leadership skills. I don't want to waste more time battling with reality."

"At least you're clear on what you don't want."

Reclaiming Your Soul's Goal

It seems easier for clients to name what they *don't* want than it is for them to dream. Somewhere along the way, they were told as children that their dreams weren't realistic. "Being an actor doesn't pay enough. You must work hard and do what's right for the family. Become a lawyer or physician." Chasing after that sort of dream is going to be a struggle because it's based on someone else's goal. Some children with vivid imaginations were told, "Grow up now and put aside those childish fantasies." Their hearts were put in cages and quieted so the mind could power through working toward other people's goals – doing what other people wanted them to do. If they see their cage doors are opened, they still sit inside afraid to venture forth. Their life force has diminished from all of the times they were told to be "realistic." It's time to rekindle that spark.

For some people, the mind chases after a seductive goal such as money or security. Employers feed that desire, luring people into jobs they don't like in companies that are not a good fit for them. They are promised a happy retirement (eventually). Money and security are not true goals; instead they're byproducts of following your soul's goal for you. In this case, it may feel dangerous to dream. You may tell yourself you don't want to even HAVE a goal. You don't want to rock the boat. Believe me: once awakened, the soul's true desire for you will eclipse your idea of safety and security. It will bring you excitement and joy in their place. Are you ready?

Your soul is here to experience life – to create, just as you were created by your parents and Spirit. You are a creator by nature and are here to experience your creations – such as your current reality. Your soul has a goal for you – to create something inspiring – and working with your Type, Strategy, and Authority will point you to it. The G Center or Identity Center is the heart of your Human Design chart where the eternal aspect of you resides. It's the home of the Magnetic Monopole – a force that attracts people and resources to you to fulfill your purpose. It's a "monopole" because it only attracts; it doesn't repel. Your Strategy and Authority are working with your G Center to point you to your goal and support you along the way. This is another powerful reason to follow your Type, Strategy, and Authority.

Fears can naturally arise when you reach for something new. For example, part of you may not want to see your true goal because you're afraid it may require you to make some hard decisions about your job or relationship. Consider this possibility: if you align with the soul's goal and allow nature to take its course, all the rest will sort itself out in the best possible way for everyone involved. Conversely, if you ignore your soul's promptings or try to control the process, the result can be a bumpy journey for you and for those impacted by your actions. Trust that your soul has the best of intentions for you and will find the optimal route. Don't allow the mind to take you on a detour.

Despite knowing this true goal, some people, choose to stay in their current realities. They've been conditioned to believe they must sacrifice for the good of the family. They take on burdens without being asked. Other family members end up feeling resentful because they see how unhappy you are. When you do what's good for you by following your inner guidance, you're naturally happier – and everyone else is too. The journey itself is joyful when you're working on your soul's goal. Sacrificing is not as noble as it sounds. Also, the mirror will happily oblige with more ways to experience self-sacrifice if that's your choice.

Make a conscious choice right now to lead your life in alignment with your soul's goal for you. Take a moment to let that sink in. Allow your mind the space it needs to come into alignment with that reality. When there is alignment with and intention to follow this Lead by Design process, your goal will manifest.

Once you set the goal, it's important not to think about exactly how to get there. The mind automatically generates plans and strategies, but don't get entangled in that. It's not your job to figure it all out. Your Type, Strategy, and Authority will lead you there. Thinking about the steps invariably surfaces many illusory problems; keep your focus on the goal.

Maggie was ready for this, so I simply said, "Let's wave a magic wand. First, wake up your inner child – she knows how to do this. Let's find your goal. Are you ready?"

"Yes." replied Maggie.

Let's find two goals – a worldly goal and a being goal. The worldly goal is something measurable – health and vitality, loving relationship, new home, successful career. A being goal is how you want to experience life. For example, "I am happy and fulfilled" or "I am empowered and confident." These types of goals can't be measured externally. Notice that they're worded in present tense. Make sure your goals are worded in present time.

Pick one worldly goal and one being goal. Don't worry if it's *the* goal. Pick one your heart leaps at.

THE *REALITY YOU PREFER* MEDITATION

Close your eyes.
Take a deep breath and release your thoughts.
This goal is not coming from your mind.
It's arising from your soul, so you can safely let go of thinking.
Take three deep conscious breaths
Keep releasing thoughts.
Tune in to your heart and connect with your higher self, with Source.
Ask for support in creating a personal goal aligned with your soul.
Relax. Breathe.
You're in the hands of Spirit.
Go back to a time when you could trust Spirit, perhaps as a young child.
Maybe you trusted your parents that way.
Maybe you talked to God, to the trees or birds.
Remember what it was like to feel and trust that connection.
Even if you had a difficult childhood, there were moments of joy, of running through grass, climbing trees.
Tune in to that child in you now
Feel in your body that lightness, that unbounding energy, curiosity,

What did this child like to do?
What did you, as this child, desire?
As you grew, what continued to attract you?
What dreams did you have?
Maybe you dreamed of being an artist, ice cream man, world-famous singer, president of a company.
Maybe you dreamed of traveling and adventures.
Be still and let your heart speak.
What dreams did you have to give up over time?
Perhaps you were told they were unrealistic.
You can't get a job as an actor.
You can't get paid well as a writer.
What dreams did you have to give up?
Do you know?
What would it be if you knew?
What dream still lights up your heart?
Can you let yourself have it?
Listen.
Don't scale back the dream.
Don't let your adult mind analyze or judge them.
Don't let the mind put limitations around it.
Allow pure fantasy here.
Enjoy the possibilities.
Dream.
No constraints.
Breathe and relax. Let the answer come to you.
What dream goal will you choose right now?
If you're a Generator – then ask, do you know your dream goal?
Choose one to play with right now.
Visualize it.
Imagine it has already happened.
See yourself living that reality now.
Does it feel exciting and uplifting, or is there tension in your body?
It's a quick response.

*Do you feel your heart singing, or is there heaviness when you see your-
self reaching this goal?*

*If there is heaviness, see if the mind has already labeled it unobtainable
or unrealistic.*

Did the mind corrupt it?

Or does the tension mean it's not your goal?

If you're a Generator, ask yes/no questions: Is this right for me?

Otherwise tune in to your guidance.

Ask for support in seeing this.

Listen.

If it's your goal write it down. If it's not your goal, choose another one.

Now tune in to your goal and reduce the importance of it.

Like you're ordering off the menu.

You're ordering an entrée.

You don't consider whether it's too big or whether it's possible.

The Universe can deliver.

You just place an order.

This is how to think about your goal.

I'll have one of those.

Visualize yourself receiving what you ordered.

If your heart feels light, keep it.

If you're feeling tension, let this one go.

Take a breath to release thoughts.

Connect with your inner child again.

Allow yourself to dream.

Allow yourself to have.

Wave a magic wand.

Just for fun, just because you can, pick another goal.

Again, tune in. Do you feel uplifted or tense?

*Don't think about how to achieve the goal or any implications of
having it.*

Let go of all of your ideas about it.

If it feels light, write it down.

Someone else's goal feels heavy, like a duty or obligation.

You have to force yourself to keep going.
Find a goal that makes your heart sing and then allow yourself to
have it.
Visualize it with resoluteness.
I'm ordering it off the menu, and I'm having it.
I don't know how I'm going to get it.
I just know it's mine and I claim it now.
Write it down.
Take a couple of energizing breaths and return your attention back to
the room.

Maggie came out of this meditation and looked at me with wide eyes.

"What did you find?"

"I'm living my dad's goal for me. I wanted to move up the corporate ladder and become a general manager or president. That's not my goal."

"What is your true goal?"

"I'm a change agent. I want to help people take charge of their lives, release old patterns and limitations, and joyfully move toward inspired goals."

"I can feel your excitement."

Maggie suddenly looked worried. "Does this mean I have to leave my job?"

"Stop right there. Remember what the mind does? It tries to figure out *how* to reach this goal and then decides it's impossible or presents you with scary scenarios. Don't listen. Trust your Inner Authority. Focus on your goal. You'll be led, one step at a time. As you think about your new goal, what is your emotional state?"

"Excited."

"Write that down. Check in again over the next couple of days as you observe your emotional wave. Then clarify who you would like to help: individuals? groups? teams in corporations? Who specifically is your new client and what would they say is the issue you're solving for them?

Through this process you'll be embodying your Human Design on a deeper level. You're now relying on your Strategy and Authority every step of the way, and you'll notice the gifts in your chart are all working for you. In your case, you're also gifted with Channel 59-06, Mating, which has the energy and capacity for creating new businesses. Tap into that energy and allow it to inform you. Get as much clarity as you can around your dream goal.

Then you can start driving toward your new destination.

8

LEARNING THE RULES OF
THE ROAD

With your true goal clarified, it's time to get into gear and out on the road. As you move in the direction of your life goals, each step on the journey feels fulfilling. This process takes awareness and practice, since your current reality keeps pulling you back in. In this chapter, you'll release some of that restraining energy and use it to reach your new destination. You'll also receive some guidance about navigating certain obstacles almost everyone encounters. Getting caught in these challenges will steer you toward a different destination with even more roadblocks. Staying awake and aware of yourself and your surroundings is key. You're traveling a new path, so don't fall asleep at the wheel.

Let's see what issues Maggie encountered on her journey.

Maggie was so inspired about the new direction she set for herself that she started working on it immediately. She clarified her goal of working with professional women with older children who wanted to scale back to part time work, to help them free up energy they could use to pursue their passions.

Her mind was working overtime laying out the steps to

reach this new goal. When she looked at the impact of taking a much lower salary while her business was growing, she freaked out and decided that perhaps this wasn't the right path for her. She was in an anxious state when we met.

"Wait a minute. Slow down. You are racing off and you're way down the road. You've already forgotten an important rule: don't let the mind tell you how to get there. It proclaims itself as an expert; however, the mind only knows how to re-create the past. Your inner guidance knows and it will only give you one step at a time. Keep following your Strategy and Authority. The mind will bring up fears because it doesn't deal well with unknowns. It doesn't know the future, but it will paint a series of frightening scenarios in an effort to protect you. It will shriek: 'Stay safe. Stay where you are. Stick with what you know. What are you thinking – going off on your own?' Meanwhile the energy field of your current life and old habits will slowly and insistently rein you back in."

Maggie nodded miserably.

"You need to be aware of your thoughts and you need extra power to escape the energy field of your current situation to get into a new orbit around your new reality."

She brightened, "Where does that extra power come from?"

"It comes from aligning with your soul and allowing it to lead you every step of the way. It comes from learning effective visualization techniques and developing new habits and attitudes. The person who has already created this goal is not the same person you are today. You can live into that now. Become the person who has already done this."

"Now you've lost me. I hear you about tuning in to my guidance for the next step and ignoring my mind's strategies. I can work on that. But becoming a different version of me? How?"

"Let's start by disempowering your current creation and

instead using your imagination to explore the new you – the one that has already created this new business."

"But I haven't created anything yet."

"Okay. I'm going to get a little esoteric here. Are you open to a new way of looking at the Universe?"

"Well, I've been open to working with the world as a Giant Reflection Field. I guess I can bring it up a notch and work with the entire Universe."

I ignored the sarcasm.

"The goal is to let the Universe work for you. Let me start at the beginning. I mean the very beginning – at the Big Bang. Everything was created in that moment – the whole Universe. Time was not part of the creation; it's just a construct that enables us to navigate our lives. But every possible scenario was created at that time. Look: I'm going to tell you a story. You don't have to believe what I am saying for these tools to work. If this resonates with you, it will help create your intentions more powerfully. Are you game?"

"Yes," said Maggie, cradling a cup of tea and settling into her chair more comfortably.

"The Universe is vast enough to contain all possibilities. Because there is infinite space, the center point is everywhere at the same time. You are the center of the Universe. Consider that for a moment: you are the center of the Universe. In fact, everyone is the center.

"You are eternal, with no beginning and no end. Your energy body continues its journey after you drop this Earth body. At some point you may even merge with the light. But even then, a drop of water that enters the ocean has not evaporated, it's still there. It has simply joined the ocean.

"Since you are without end, time doesn't exist. Take that in for a moment.

"Since every point is the center of the Universe, everything in the Universe exists right now. Your past, present, and future all exist right now. Everything exists in the present moment. Everything is happening concurrently. The present is here. The past is here now. You know this because you keep living it, replaying victim stories or hurtful incidents in your mind. Your future is also here now. Scientists are just beginning to learn more about this, but your future reality is already manifested in a huge variety of ways. Your future is not predetermined, and no one can accurately predict it. All possible variations of your future exist right now – but not in the physical sense of parallel worlds. The information about all possible futures exists in an information space. The version of you that became president of the company is in the information field and you can access it. The version of you that lives alone, the one that's married with kids – all of these exist somewhere.

"You're currently living out one of these versions. You'll continue on your current trajectory until you make a shift. For example, a shift in consciousness may put you in a higher trajectory where there is more success in your life. On the other hand, if you persist in negativity, guilt, and resentment, you will shift to a lower trajectory where you experience more of that in your life. You're on a current life path, but what you think, say and do can move you into a different one.

"Are you still with me?"

Maggie nodded, intrigued.

"You may have an intention that you know you can achieve, and it's likely on your current path. You just want to get there now. Or you may have a stretch goal such as the one you're considering, that is likely not on your current path. This is where you call on a higher power for support. Call on your inner guidance to take you there. I'll guide you through the steps of manifesting. Both realities exist *now* and both are accessible.

"So, when you start visualizing your new goal, know that

it already exists somewhere in this vast Universe. Your visualization lights up this scenario in the information space and breathes life into it. Your life path starts to slowly shift to this one. Believing this reality already exists gives you a higher level of confidence and empowers the process. You don't have to work on your conviction level if you believe that all possibilities exist now. Your mind can more easily accept the goal and align with your soul's intention. There is a relief in just knowing it's already done. Now, you can order off the menu.

"Your ability to hold this visualization in consciousness and manifest a switch to the new life path takes skill. We can work on this together. A regular meditation practice is key to training your attention and building awareness. You have two levers you can work with – intention and attention. Training your attention to concentrate on the reality you prefer is one key to Manifesting and leading your life in the direction of your goal.

"At higher levels of consciousness this becomes easier. David Hawkins MD, PhD, a renowned authority within the fields of consciousness research and spirituality, has written and taught from the unique perspective of an experienced clinician, scientist, and mystic. He spoke about simply holding something in his consciousness and then seeing it manifest quickly. For example, he would hold in mind the location of an event where he was scheduled to speak, not knowing the directions. Invariably he would drive the car straight to his destination. This worked for him because he was in a high state of consciousness.

Although you can't just move yourself into a higher level of consciousness, you can work on directing your attention, which can build more awareness, and help you accomplish things you have only dreamed about. Your ability to monitor and align with specific thoughts, words, and actions is important for moving onto higher trajectories that are more fulfilling for you.

"Now, since you've already successfully created this new business in some version of reality, you can help yourself manifest that by becoming that version of you. Use your imagination and adopt the posture, thoughts, and attitudes of the you that is on that trajectory. Work with that and with visualizing your goal, until these skills become strong enough for you to escape the energy field of your old self and align more sustainably with the new one. Keep watching your thoughts."

Maggie stirred, "That was a long trip to the punch line. I need to imitate this new version of me. You've always taught me to be authentic. Now you want me to fake it?"

"You're upgrading your habits, attitudes, and actions, but you're still maintaining your core identity. You're following your soul's desire. Developing a new habit can feel uncomfortable and inauthentic until it's integrated into your life. If you take actions in accordance with that new reality, the world mirror will reflect it back to you. It takes time to create new habits and to see a shift. Be patient.

"If the new habits and attitudes seem too much of a stretch for you, I can support you in addressing that. There are a few life hacks that can get you into a new comfort zone."

Maggie nodded, lost in thought. "Thank you, but I believe I can do this."

"Perfect.

"That was a lot to digest. Let's review and then release the power of your current reality through an experiential process. Get comfortable again."

PROCESS TO RELEASE YOUR CURRENT REALITY
AND MOVE TOWARD YOUR PREFERRED ONE

Look at the worldly goal you wrote down for yourself.
At the moment you adopt it, see how it feels in your body.
Say it out loud to yourself from a place of claiming it as your goal and feel your response.
If there is tension, investigate if this is your goal.
There can be discomfort, but the overall feeling should be uplifting.
Then the heart and mind can align.
Breathe.
Now close your eyes and slow down your breathing.
Move your attention to the heart area.
Consciously connect with your higher self or Source.
Breathe.
You should feel lighter or more expansive.
If not, then stop and take a few minutes to move your energy. Put on music and dance, or chant, or do some yoga postures.
Relax into your heart space and breathe.
Now bring your attention to your current reality – including any hidden details uncovered by the alien in our previous meditation.
Take a few moments to observe all of it from a place of curiosity.
Now, accept all of it by simply acknowledging its right to exist.
Remember that you created this version of reality with thoughts, words, and actions.
Take ownership for your creation.
Hold it lightly.
You may notice how it's using your energy to stay alive.
Simply release the energy or put your creation on a cloud and let it float away.
Feel the space that has been opened up inside.
Look at your new intention.
Know that your new reality already exists somewhere in the Universe.

Visualize it here now.

See yourself as a participant in the visualization.

You're not an observer but rather an actor in the movie.

Act your part – adopt the posture, attitude, and viewpoint of the you that has already created this.

Walk around in your creation.

Feel the joy and sense of fulfillment.

Now, release it.

Tune in to your guidance.

If you're a Generator or Manifesting Generator, ask yourself:

Is there an action step for you to take now?

For other Types:

What is my next step?

Open your eyes, write it down and commit to doing it.

As Maggie finished writing, I reminded her, "Don't listen to any steps that come from your mind. Be patient and stay aware. When you're complete with a step, ask your guidance for the next step. Use your Type, Strategy, and Authority to navigate. With each new piece of evidence that your new creation is unfolding, celebrate. Your experience of reality will shift.

I'll help you develop the skills needed to move through this process in a powerful way and when you're ready, we'll upgrade your visualization."

Maggie left the room with more determination and a lightness in her step.

This process was focused on a worldly goal. I think you can already guess how to work with your being goal. If your goal is to be happy and fulfilled, what do you do? Stand in front of the mirror. Be happy and fulfilled. Also, make someone else feel happy and fulfilled. Give what it is you want to receive. It works every time.

UNIVERSAL ROADBLOCKS

As you navigate toward the direction you have set for yourself, you'll invariably encounter certain universal roadblocks. You're probably clear about the danger of aligning with negativity, but there are other more insidious attitudes that can send you into a long detour. Some major ones are guilt, inferiority/ superiority, seriousness, self-sacrifice, and being unable to receive. You'd be surprised how often these thoughts hijack your attention, especially when they attach to your conditioning creating a story you believe. It's part of human nature to get caught in these attitudes, and it takes awareness to see them and choose differently. Let's look at how inferiority triggered Jackie's conditioning and how she worked with it.

When I first started working with Jackie, she carried a deep sense of inferiority or not being good enough. Her mother died when she was young, and on some level, she felt it was her fault. There was no rational reason for this feeling. As a young child, she reacted emotionally and kept saying to herself, "If only I were better, my mom wouldn't have left me." She overcompensated for this sense of lack by working too hard, and it was exhausting her. As a Generator, she has sustainable energy, but she often has trouble saying *no* to requests. With The Gate of Power, Gate 34 (see Chart C), this problem can be magnified, leading to burnout. I worked with her to surface and release this sabotaging belief, "I'm not good enough," from her childhood. She was able to stop blaming herself. However, from the long years of carrying this program in her subconscious, there was a lingering sense of inferiority. Her goals would continue to elude her as long as she allowed this feeling to a gain a foothold.

Inferiority is a common universal roadblock, and it includes superiority, as the other side of the same coin. Both will send you on a detour. It's natural to want to feel significant, as this is one of the basic needs of the mind. How you deal with it is the issue. We're bombarded with media programming us to believe in the perfect body type, attitude, lifestyle, relationships. Of course, you come up short by comparison; everyone does. When you strive to fit some ideal or image in your brain, you abandon yourself and the many gifts you naturally carry. Your heart can never align behind a goal to be someone you're not. All the time you're standing in front of the mirror, asking for significance, the mirror is intensifying your need for more significance.

When Jackie stopped comparing herself to others and started following specific protocols, she released that sense of inferiority. The world mirror reflected back to her that all was well and this reinforced her sense of wholeness. Suddenly people acknowledged her more and asked her opinions on various issues. Her ability to engage successfully at work improved substantially.

Guilt is perhaps the biggest roadblock and one that practically everyone encounters, since it's deeply ingrained in our current culture. Guilt has been used by teachers, religious authorities and parents since childhood to manipulate us into behaving in certain ways. It comes with the belief that "If you're guilty you must do as I say." To understand just how dangerous aligning with this energy can be, stand in front of a mirror. Put on your best guilty face and look at the image from a place of detachment. What would you say about this person? The first thing that pops into my mind is that they did something wrong. Next my mind starts looking for what they could have done – and it usually finds something. Keep looking at this guilty face in the mirror. What else do you notice? They're asking to be punished. An energetic signal is going out to anyone who would like to pick up on it – "please punish me." The mirror will oblige, and someone will show up in your life to deliver your request. At that point you might move into a state of victimhood. "Why does this always happen to me?" Since there's a delay between feeling guilty and receiving punishment, there's no sense of accountability. The victim has plenty of evidence that it's someone else's fault. While I'm not condoning the behavior of the aggressor, the real cause of this punishment is your guilty conscience.

When Sandra contacted me, she related a series of unfortunate incidents that had plagued her over the last few months. It turned out her older sister Vanessa had come for a visit three months ago, and they had talked about old times. In their childhood their parents were strict and especially tough on her older sister. She got into trouble if any of the younger children misbehaved. When Sandra would make a mistake, her sister would come down on her so hard and fast she became traumatized. Sandra has a 1/3 learning Profile that requires her to make mistakes, because she learns by trial and error. Since mistakes were punished so swiftly in her household, she thought something was seriously wrong with her. She walked around feeling like she was a mistake. Over the years, she had learned to let go of that feeling, but when her sister visited, it surfaced those old wounds. She fell back into the habit of experiencing guilt, which led to a series of unfortunate events, including having her wallet stolen.

As long as she continues to take the stance that "I've done something wrong so I must be punished," she will continue to invite attacks. Your heart and soul never align with punishment, so this experience is clearly coming from conditioning or old beliefs.

There are many forms of guilt and as Sandra worked through various processes, she was able to reclaim her sense of wholeness. In some cases, it was enough to stop justifying her actions. In other situations, she needed to make amends and do some forgiveness work. Eventually she started feeling that all was right with the world. The mirror reflected this back to her. The unfortunate accidents stopped, and she was once again leading her life.

Guilt is insidious. Recently I was working with some community members on this issue. Since it was forefront in my mind, I started noticing places where I still hold guilt on a subtle level. For example, I messaged a client that I would be ten minutes late for our call and asked if that was okay. She agreed. When I got on the call, I started to go into the story of why I needed an extra ten minutes. I caught myself experiencing guilt and stopped talking for a moment. I realized my attention was on myself. I tuned into my client and thought about what she might want to hear from me. Instead of explaining myself I told her how grateful I was for those extra ten minutes and thanked her. She didn't want to hear my stories, and she happily received the compliment.

Guilt keeps you focused on yourself rather than the other person. It crops up in the most unexpected times. Stay aware and awake.

Before we move on, let's look briefly at a couple of other common roadblocks – seriousness and self-sacrifice. Where there is seriousness, there is judgment or fear, and the mind has taken hold of you. About twenty-five years ago, my husband and I trekked to the Mount Everest basecamp with a group from REI. Along the way we visited a high Lama in a remote Himalayan village. He blessed us on our journey and tied red prayer strings around each of us. When I remember our visit, I remember his laughter. Even when he wasn't laughing, he looked like he was ready to do so. It made a deep impact on me. Many years later when spiritual masters visited our center, they would remind us that seriousness closes down access to our guidance and to higher order processes such as compassion. As the Bible says, "Wear the world as a light garment," and you'll have a better perspective. Life is a game, and it takes focus and commitment to move through it consciously, not seriously.

When you think about self-sacrifice, what could be more serious than that? We've already talked about its effect on you and the ones you're trying to help. There's a particular way this roadblock interferes with your goals. Part of self-sacrifice is not allowing yourself to have what you truly want. I find this program is running in many of my clients, and you can imagine how it stops you from creating the reality you prefer. As soon as you become aware that it's operating, you can you choose differently. Your soul wants to fulfill your desires, so "not allowing yourself to have" is an idea originating from your conditioning. Tap into the heart and reconnect with the joy of receiving. If it's still an issue, we can work through it.

A WARNING ABOUT OBSTACLES AND ROADBLOCKS

Now that you're trained to look for these obstacles, don't think of them as obstacles! You might say, "But you trained me!" Yes, that's true but it was simply to get your attention. I needed to increase their importance so you would listen and take it *seriously* and now you that have done so, drop their importance! Be serious only about your commitment to controlling your attention. Remember that if you focus on obstacles, the world mirror will show you more of them. Instead, learn to see road-blocks as simply part of your journey. Then the mirror will reflect progress toward your goal. Better still, find the silver lining in every obstacle and savor that. Trust me – there's always an upside in this duality. Get creative.

When you think of inferiority as an *obstacle*, it keeps your focus on the problem rather than the solution. Most of us tend to become enamored of our problems. The mind loves to do this because it generates a lot of thinking. Problems draw you in by appearing highly complex, but simple solutions are always available. You can safely drop this bad habit. For example, a simple fix (not necessarily easy) for feeling inferior or superior is to stop comparing. Solutions like this one are never found by thinking about the problem. Instead, they're found by becoming still and asking for guidance. Since all possibilities exist in this vast Universe, your solution already exists. Your Inner Authority will point the way.

In summary, when you meet your next obstacle, treat it as another cobblestone on your path. Tune in to your guidance and direct your attention to the solution. Do this without making it important. Also, be sure to acknowledge the silver lining in the situation.

I experienced the beauty of dropping importance on the El Camino walk. One day, while walking from Coimbra to Mealhada, Portugal, we experienced drenching rains three to four times a day, with each shower lasting about twenty minutes. I've never seen so much rain pouring out of the sky. The streets became rivers. After each downpour, the sun would come out, and we'd dry out as we walked. My inner guidance told me to keep going. So, we continued our journey and eventually arrived at our destination in good shape. Later we found out that Coimbra had been hit by a hurricane. Because we didn't know this, we didn't make it bigger than it was; it was simply part of our path, and we dealt with each shower good-naturedly as it arrived. Had I known that it was a *hurricane*, it might have become a big *obstacle* in my mind, and I might not have walked that day or I may have walked in fear. In this case, the world mirror reflected back that all was well, and it was.

On your journey, become aware of all your bad habits – including your preference for bad news. As you start tracking your attention, you'll find yourself automatically gravitating toward bad news; meanwhile, good news gets a fleeting nod.

This happens in the blink of an eye, and you may miss it. What will the mirror reflect back to you? Clearly you prefer bad news, so you'll receive more of it.

Recently I watched the 100 Foot Wave TV series because I had just returned from visiting Nazaré, Portugal. The surfers who successfully rode waves over seventy feet high were spectacular to watch. However, on Instagram, they received nowhere near the number of likes as the footage of wipeouts. This just shows that we're wired for danger and we have some serious reprogramming to do to get you on a successful trajectory! The saber-toothed tiger is not going to devour you like it did our ancestors; negative thoughts, on the other hand, just might. Stay awake and aware. Learn to savor the pleasant thoughts and experiences in life.

I recommend periodically using the Letting Go process in Appendix F to train yourself to release these feelings when you encounter them and to do some gentle clearing.

Be sure to handle rogue thoughts that trigger you as soon as they arise so you can continue traveling to your desired destination.

9

RELEASING LIMITATIONS AND LEVERAGING YOUR STRENGTHS

Take a moment to tune back in to the life goal that you uncovered in Chapter 6 and visualized in Chapter 7. Does it inspire you? Does it also bring up fear or concern about your ability to step into it? Are you still waiting for the guidance on your next step?

Gather your Human Design chart and your journal or paper and pen. It's time to go deeper in your chart, align with your strengths, release sabotaging patterns, and identify the places you may be giving your power away. Based on my design, I'm here to support leaders to realize their big dreams, evolve within the context of limitations or transcend them and to write a new leadership story. Your dream is your life goal, and we're currently working with the one you have already written down. One of your major limiting factors is the conditioning that exists in your Centers. These are other people's ideas, values, feelings and fears that you've absorbed without examining them, and they are leading your life. In this chapter, you'll surface and release limiting beliefs and receive a deeper appreciation of the gifts that you already possess. From this new level of clarity, you can revisit your goal and tweak it if necessary. In Chapter 10 you'll write a new leadership story for yourself.

OPENNESS AND DEFINITION REVISITED

In Chapter 4 we briefly explored the functions and themes of the nine Centers as well as the differences between Defined and Open Centers. In the last chapter, you saw how Jackie's conditioning caused her pain. At an early age, she took on the belief "I'm not good enough," which likely landed in her Open Head Center. Now, let's go deeper into the Centers in your chart to discover the source of your pain points. We'll surface conditioned beliefs that are in the way of your goal so you can feel more freedom. To do this, you'll need to deepen your understanding of Openness and Definition. Are you ready?

Look at your own chart as we go through the Centers so you can begin to integrate all this information. Centers become Defined when there is a red and/ or black Channel connecting them. Remember that not only do you have consistent access to the energies in a Defined Center, but you're also constantly broadcasting that energy. For example, my client Jackie (refer to Chart C) has three Defined Centers, Sacral, Root, and Spleen Centers, with Channel 27-50, Preservation, and Channel 53-42, The Channel of Maturation, connecting them. She has consistent access to the following energies: the adrenalized energy in the Root Center, which helps her get started on projects; sustainable energy in the Sacral Center; and her intuition in the Spleen Center. While these energies are always available to her, she can misuse them. For example, with Gate 29, Perseverance, Jackie can easily say yes to too many requests that are a no for her. Her Sacral motor turns off, and she experiences burnout or lack of sustainable energy. As long as she's aligned with her Type, Strategy, and Authority, Jackie has access to sustainable energy and to the gifts of this Gate, which include being able to persevere through projects or challenges in a committed relationship.

Your Open Centers are fluid, absorbing the energies of others or your environment, and amplifying them. Since you don't have consistent access to the specific energies of those Centers, you're here to explore all their various qualities. You can be more versatile or flexible in your thinking, feeling or energy. Another gift of this openness is an ability to take in or merge with others in these Centers. For example, you might merge with them in the Head Center, truly understanding their point of view, or you may take in their feelings from the Emotional Solar Plexus and feel their passion. If you can stay in the openness, you may experience a taste of oneness with others or the world around you.

The mind, uncomfortable with the fluidity, coopts this process by fixating on certain beliefs, values or fears, and causing you to blindly adopt them. This may initially give you a sense of security. However, this is how conditioning arises – you take on other people's ideas and patterns without realizing it or examining them. As a result, your life unfolds according to their beliefs, values, feelings, and so on. In other words, someone else is leading your life.

In Maggie's case, she realized she had adopted her dad's idea of which career was best for her. Until she examined this, she thought it was her idea. With Open Centers, you need to stay aware and discern which beliefs, feelings, values, energies, and fears actually belong to you. Ask yourself, "Am I feeling anger right now or is someone near me angry? "

We'll focus here on surfacing and releasing some of the conditioned beliefs that are not aligned with your new direction. This type of clearing is an ongoing process because conditioning is possible whenever you're operating on automatic or unconsciously. When you're awake and aware, you can avoid taking on other people's ideas. As you focus more on your awareness, you'll realize how fleeting it can be. Suddenly you may find that your mind has drifted and you're on automatic again. Without a consistent meditation practice, you haven't become practiced at controlling your attention. The more aware you become, the more you'll realize just how often you're asleep. We'll work with training your attention in the next chapter. For now though, it's important to understand the extent to which you've taken on conditioning. We're limiting our present focus to the beliefs that are in the way of your current goal.

Some people have a lot of Definition in their design, and they still have clearing to do. Anyone with all nine Centers Defined has a solid sense of themselves and is not so easily influenced by others. Their conditioning primarily lands in their Open Channels and Open Gates. If you have one of these rare designs, you can still use the processes in this chapter to surface them. Reflectors on the other hand are completely fluid in all respects with their nine Open Centers. Their challenge is to give themselves time to integrate all the information they're receiving, so they can make effective decisions. They may be more aware and less likely to take on conditioning than another Type with several Open Centers. Their main focus is to cultivate the witness state and come into the present moment, where they have an amazing ability to move into a state of Oneness. Although in this state they're not vulnerable to conditioning. Reflectors would still benefit from looking at their conditioning.

CENTERS REVISITED

Let's look at Definition and Openness from the point of view of each Center so you can get a sense of its impact on the various themes. This is a vast field of exploration, so we're just skimming the surface. This list is mainly for reference, but note any insights as you read through it. You'll have a chance to more deeply consider your Centers in the meditations later in this chapter. For now, note any differences you observe between your Defined and Open Centers. Also note if your experience of a particular Center is markedly different from the description here. You likely have some conditioning to clear in that Center. For now, just enjoy the exploration and stay curious.

HEAD CENTER

Center of inspiration, thoughts, and ideas and one of the pressure centers in the chart – the pressure to know.

People with Defined Head Centers comprise 57 percent of the population. They're broadcasting thoughts and ideas, so their minds are constantly active; they know what they think. Consequently, they tend to have limited ability to consider various points of view.

An Open Head Center, on the other hand, is taking in ideas and amplifying them. People with this design are not fixated on a particular viewpoint but are open to all viewpoints and ideas; unless they are conditioned to believe they should have fixed ideas. They may not remember things and, therefore, think something is wrong with them. Often they'll have an impression of something they have experienced rather than remembering specific details. Since the Head Center is also a pressure center, they feel pressured to come up with answers.

While I was growing up, everyone in my family, except possibly my sister had an Open Head and Ajna. My mother had a photographic memory, which is also another possibility for people with an Open Head. Both of my children also have an Open Head and Ajna, so when my partner (with a Defined Head and Ajna) started living with us, I could feel a dramatic

difference. I just didn't have the language for it. Now I understand why my mind is busy around him and why he is always
certain of his viewpoints and knows where he stands on
issues. I admired that quality and adopted the belief that "I
should know what I think," but often I didn't. When I felt his
certainty, I would take on his viewpoint to stop feeling wishy-
washy, but it didn't help. I had to learn to be okay with not
knowing in his presence and not to take his certainty as a sign
that his opinion was right for me. It took a while for me to
learn to simply rest in the openness of my Head Center.

AJNA CENTER

*Center for conceptualizing, processing, and interpreting opinions and
answers.*

People with Defined Ajna Centers comprise 47 percent of
the population. They have consistent access to processing the
information from their Head Center and so they're always
thinking. They process differently depending on which Gates
are Defined. They're designed to be certain but not always
right. They're not easily influenced and may at times pressure
others to think in alignment with them.

People with an Open Ajna are designed to be more flexible
in their thinking. Since they're not designed to be certain,
they may have a fear of looking stupid. In this case, they may
also be conditioned to believe they should be certain. While
they may not be able to process information in a reliable way,
sometimes, I notice, they're very creative in their methods of
processing data.

THROAT CENTER

Center for communication and manifestation.

This Center is a focal point; all the energy in the chart is trying to get to the Throat for expression. This Center directly connects to every other Center except for the Head and Root, and it contains more Gates than any other Center. You can think of it as the town square or the central hub of activity. Through the Throat Center we express ideas, creativity, intuitive messages, feelings, love and power. Our leadership is expressed through our voice, so it's critical to know how to properly work with it. The energy is rushing here because when we have the energetic connection of a motor to the Throat, manifestation is possible. We are fundamentally creators and have a deep-seated need to be heard. The creation of our Universe began with a sound – *In the beginning was the Word.* We continue to create and impact others through our words and actions.

People with Defined Throats comprise 72 percent of the population. They have consistent access to their voice and a sense of confidence that comes with that gift. They also have a consistent way of speaking that takes on different flavors depending on which Channel connects to the Throat Center. For example, someone with the Channel 22-12, Openness, can speak with depth about the human experience when they are in the mood. A little over half of the people with Defined Throats have a motor connected to their Throat (Manifestors and Manifesting Generators). They have the gift of manifesting when they're operating according to their Strategy and Authority.

People with an Open Throat are looking for an energetic connection with someone who has a motor to the Throat Center in order to manifest. Their biggest challenge is being heard, because they have to wait for an invitation or be acknowledged to speak. They may try to attract attention, or they might push through to be heard and then wonder why their wisdom falls on deaf ears. It's vitally important for them to follow their Strategy and Authority, both in terms of right timing in their speaking and for guiding the conversation. Some people with an Open Throat tend to blurt things out or speak at length once someone is listening to them. They need to place some attention on the listener for a cue of when to slow down or stop.

You might have a sense that leaders with an Open Throat have a particular conundrum, especially when they believe they should speak up or initiate conversations. They have to wait for an invitation or recognition rather than speak when they have an idea or impulse to do so. However, when speaking in alignment with their design, they have powerful gifts. They can speak spontaneously, allowing the unknown to come through. Their voice has range and capacity, and their tone and modulation naturally adjusts to meet people where they are. When speaking to a crowd, listeners might feel as if they're *speaking directly to them.*

My brother is a highly successful lawyer with an Open Throat that commands the room when he's invited to speak. He has always had the ability to imitate voices and to deliver just the right statement at the perfect time to impact the room. In 1967 he was invited to be on the Dating Game, a popular TV show. In this game, a bachelorette asks questions of the three bachelors hidden behind a screen on stage to determine which one she wants to date. In response to one of her questions, my brother dropped into the voice of the prison Captain speaking to Paul Newman in the movie classic, *Cool Hand Luke,* saying "What we've got here is failure to communicate." The audience loved it and of course he was chosen to go on the date with her.

G OR IDENTITY CENTER

Center for love, identity, direction in life, higher self, or magnetic monopole.

The G Center is the heart of the design, holding the whole chart together as a Magnetic Monopole. It's through this Center that your higher self attracts people, situations, and resources to support you in following your direction in life. People with a Defined Identity Center comprise 57 percent of the population. They're blessed with many gifts, including a strong sense of self and direction in life. They also can have a sense of being loved and being lovable. Since they're so solid in themselves, they may expect others to follow them, especially if they're not following their Authority.

People with an Open G are fluid in their identities, and they walk through the world in such a radically different way than people with a Defined G. They face a particular conundrum when it comes to leadership: if they're conditioned to believe that a leader shows up as being *somebody*, then they may feel lost in that role. They're not designed to be *somebody* but rather to be whomever they are in the moment without attachment. They can easily move between their roles as boss, mother, and lover, without identifying with any of them. They get their identity from their environment rather than what they do, so it's important that their surroundings feel good to them. My mother would always ask for a different table at the restaurant or to change hotel rooms if she didn't like the view. I do that too. People with an Open G tend to question their lovability and are here to learn that they are Love. That can be a profound journey. They often lack a sense of direction and instead, need to trust they will be shown the way, through following their Type, Strategy, and Authority. If they can learn to surrender to this way of operating, they can be that inspired leader that is led by the higher self. In fact, they can lead as strongly – if not even more powerfully –than someone with a Defined G who has a strong sense of themselves.

I have an Open G Center, and I remember as a child and teenager trying to figure out who I was. Everyone had their ideas about me – bright student, athletic, reserved. I rejected all these labels because I couldn't feel them. When college professors spoke highly of me, I felt like a fraud and said "they just don't know me." The truth was that I just didn't know me. I remember as a child, overhearing a conversation between my brother and sister about what I would look like when I was older. They were flipping through a magazine. How I longed to get my hands on that magazine to see who I was going to be. That longing never left. I felt like the baby bird in the children's book that keeps asking all the animals, "Are you my mother?" only I kept asking everyone in various indirect ways, "Do you know who I am?" It wasn't until later in life when I had come to terms with the fact that I'd never get my identity from what I did that I started relaxing into the space of openness and let it be. I now cherish that fluidity. Human Design gave me the language for what I had experienced and validated he importance of my surroundings. I've always surrounded myself with beauty – artwork, flowers, candles.

WILL CENTER

Center for will power, navigating the material world, self-esteem, value.

People with Defined Will Centers comprise only 12 percent of the population. They can be counted on to do what they say they're going to do. They tend to recognize their value and sometimes even inflate it. They like to be *in control* of life (for example, choosing when and where they work) and of all their resources.

People with an Open Will Center are not designed to commit and do what they say they're going to do. Instead, they're here to explore what they value. They may question their value and can overachieve to compensate. They're here to learn that they don't have to prove their value.

This was shocking to me – that people wouldn't necessarily value doing what they say they're going to do. Yes, I have a Defined Will. I used to think clients needed motivational support, more direction or time management skills. Human Design gave me a completely new understanding and more effective strategies to support people. I've had Projector clients with Defined Will Centers who follow through to the point of overextending themselves. They need support with following their Strategy and Authority. Conversely, I've had Generator clients with plenty of sustainable energy not following through because they valued other things instead, like time with family. They also need to follow their Strategy and Authority at the initial commitment stage. When they look at what they value and link it to completing that project, they're more successful.

SACRAL CENTER

Center for sustainable energy.

People with a Defined Sacral Center comprise 70 percent of the population. These are the Generators and Manifesting Generators who have consistent access to this energy if they're following their inner GPS. Overriding their *no* responses leads to burnout. They're driven to find the best use of this energy toward their personal goals and must be in response rather than initiating.

People with Open Sacral Centers lack sustainable energy and the internal GPS, and they belong to one of three Types – Manifestors, Projectors, or Reflectors. As you may remember from the overview of the five Types in Chapter 5, they take in and amplify the energy of others and must be careful to monitor that so they don't overdo things and burn out.

They're sensitive to the energy levels in other people and their environment and they need time to rest, away from the Generator field.

ROOT CENTER

Center for physical adrenalized pressure, sustaining momentum, stress, as well as a pressure center – the pressure to do something.

People with a Defined Root Center comprise 60 percent of the population. They have a fixed way of dealing with stress. They're grounded and have access to the energy of starting projects, and they need to use their Strategy and Authority to start appropriately.

People with an Open Root Center feel under pressure to do something. They're absorbing stress from the environment and want to dissipate it through action (which doesn't work). They need to learn to discern what is theirs to do and allow the pressure. They may feel ungrounded and have trouble starting projects.

I recently supported Patrick, a young professional, through a transitional time when he was confused and making impulsive decisions that were creating havoc in his life (refer to Chart I in the Appendix). He needed a job quickly and wanted to move from Chicago to Arizona. In a place of fear, he was accepting jobs in Arizona that weren't the best fit for him and then regretting his decision and backing out of them. He starting doubting himself with even simple, everyday decisions after experiencing the pain of accepting and then rejecting multiple jobs.

He learned to work with his yes/no decision-making and to take the time to come to a space of neutrality. Still he felt the pressure to act. Patrick was also dealing with an Open Root Center and a Triple Split Definition, which were both intensifying his need to do something quickly. You'll notice he has eight Defined Centers and one Open Center – the Root. This Center operates like an ignition switch. It turns on the engine so that the Sacral motor can run. As the Root Center pulsed on and off, Patrick kept feeling intense pressure to do something. However, doing something just to relieve pressure didn't work, and he became very anxious. He had to learn to allow the pressure and use his Strategy and Authority to decide.

His Triple Split Definition magnified the problem for him. Remember (from our brief overview in Chapter 4) that a Triple Split means that his Defined Centers are in three groupings. He's looking at the issue first with his Head and Ajna Centers; then with his Spleen, Will Center, G Center, and Emotional Solar Plexus; and finally with the Sacral and Throat Centers. It takes time to integrate the information from these various Center groupings, and people with this Definition tend toward impulsiveness. The pressure to decide in the moment was particularly intense for Patrick. Once he understood where this pressure was coming from and why he felt pushed into action, he was finally able to stop and commit to aligning with his design. With support he slowed down, came to a solid decision, and moved to Arizona.

EMOTIONAL SOLAR PLEXUS

Center for feelings, passion, sensitivity, creativity, and spirit awareness.

People with a Defined Emotional Solar Plexus comprise 53 percent of the population. They receive clarity in decision-making over time or from a place of neutrality. They're constantly riding a wave of emotions, moving away from pain and toward pleasure. Even if they feel numb, that's a feeling state, and it's a different experience from people with an Open Emotional Solar Plexus (ESP). People with a Defined

Emotional Solar Plexus impact the room with their emotional state.

People with an Open ESP are taking in and amplifying the feelings in their environment. Since they're generally even-keeled in their emotions, this can be challenging. They generally don't like big feelings. They need to discern if what they're feeling is theirs, and if not, they can leave the room to escape that field.

I have an Open ESP and have a reputation for being calm even in the midst of chaos. Both of my parents had a Defined ESP, and as a child, I would hide in my room when their emotions were running high, unable to deal with it. Despite the fact they never argued in my presence, I could feel the emotions they were suppressing. Later in life, I learned various strategies for dealing with big emotional energy. When my partner, who has a Defined ESP, became angry, I would either stay present to the feeling and let it run through me or react.

When my teacher, Robin explained that I could just walk out of the room, and it would go away, I realized I had dismissed this strategy from my childhood. I was astounded at how well it worked. It's like stepping out of a rainstorm. Usually, my partner realizes that his anger is not directed at me, so there is no harm in leaving the room. Also it's much easier for me than standing in the rain.

SPLEEN CENTER

Center for awareness, intuition, survival/ fear, health and well-being, immune system, and time.

People with a Defined Spleen comprise 55 percent of the population. They project a state of well-being, so they're grounding for people with an Open Spleen to be around. They have consistent access to their intuition. With their survival instincts, they operate in the now or present moment, searching for any danger in the environment. There is a sense of always being on alert because threat signals happen in the moment and can't be missed. It's not like an alarm clock that repeats the warning until you take action; you have to hear that still, small voice in the moment.

People with an Open Spleen are taking in and amplifying the fears of others, so they need to learn to face their fears. Each time they face them, strength builds, and this can lead to an experience of fearlessness and well-being. They may also experience health issues with their immune system, and energy healing modalities tend to work best for them. People with Open Spleens are attracted to those with a Defined Spleen, much like someone with a Small Split is attracted to someone who makes them feel whole. However, they need to follow their Type, Strategy, and Authority to reduce any co-dependency and to find and maintain healthy relationships.

Since the Spleen operates in the now, it has an interesting relationship with time. People with Defined Spleens have a natural sense of timing and tend to be on time for appointments. I have a Defined Spleen and always know what time it is, without checking my phone. People with an Open Spleen tend to lose track of time and are often late. Some of them compensate for this by always arriving early to a meeting. If someone is usually late for appointments with you, don't take it personally.

My Defined Spleen has five of the seven Gates Defined, so fear has been a constant companion for me. While growing up I kept thinking something bad was going to happen or something was wrong with me because I was feeling so afraid. I didn't observe this level of fear in others. So I reacted by being courageous and trying new things. I became an avid roller coaster rider and experimented with skydiving in an effort to conquer that fear. Later, through many spiritual trainings, I was able to allow the fear and keep my attention on what I was doing. Fear no longer defined me or had power over me. Human Design confirmed for me that I do have consistent access to several different flavors of fear, but I now appreciate the gifts that comes with it – a strong intuition and an alertness in the present moment.

As you were reading about each of these Centers and looking at your chart, what stood out for you? Did you discover anything new? Can you sense a difference between Definition and Openness in your Centers?

Let's return to Maggie's situation and see how this knowledge supported her.

MAGGIE'S JOURNEY

Maggie was tuning in to her guidance and moving toward her new goal of working with women who wanted to shift to part time work and focus on their passions. She started meeting with various advisors as she put her business plan together. While the excitement of being in action was still there, she began to have doubts again.

Maggie was pacing the room, talking excitedly. "I don't know who to believe. Kathy says my target market is too small, and that I should leverage my experience by working with businesses. I can see her point, but something doesn't quite feel right. One of my other advisors likes my plan but thinks I should create workshops for large audiences instead of working with small groups. I see her point and think maybe I should do that. Jeanette wants me to offer live events, and Kathy says online is the way to go. There are a million decisions and I feel so wishy-washy because I keep saying, 'I agree' to everyone I'm talking with. Then when I refocus, I'm not so sure. Have I lost my ability to function?"

I pulled out her Human Design (Chart D) and pointed to

her totally Open Head and Ajna Centers. By "totally Open," I mean she has no Gates Defined in those Centers.

"Remember that with your Open Head and Ajna, you are taking in ideas from everyone, and you're not designed to be certain. There is pressure to know in that Head Center, and yet you don't. Also, when you try to express your point of view, there's no connection between the Ajna and the Throat, so you may not always be able to voice those ideas during the conversation. Now, the beauty of your Open Head is that you can meld with anyone and truly understand their point of view. Hence, you keep agreeing with everyone and you're sincere about it. It's important for you to discern what you yourself actually believe. Ask yourself, 'Am I operating from other people's ideas of what I should do or from my own?'"

"How do I decide what to do?"

"Remember not to make decisions from your Head. It's a Center for inspiration and gathering ideas. The Ajna organizes and examines those ideas, but decisions are always made based on your Type, Strategy, and Authority. First come to a place of neutrality and then ask yourself yes/no questions about these different options you've received. If the answers aren't coming, it may not be time yet to decide."

Maggie sighed, "How did I lose sight of that? I know to follow my Authority."

I nodded empathetically. "When there is pressure to know in the Head Center and you don't know, the mind gets agitated and tries to fill in missing information or solve a problem for you that doesn't even exist. The mind is uncomfortable sitting in the unknown or waiting for answers. Remember, the mind is only able to repeat old patterns, so its answers won't take you into your new reality. But it can become loud and noisy at times, and it can be hard to ignore. In those moments stop, breathe, and remember that your internal guidance has much more information available to it.

Your soul can even see a little into the future – like those car mirrors that can peer around blind corners."

Maggie was repeating to herself like a mantra: "I remember. Be in response. Ask yes/no questions while tracking my emotional wave. Guidance will come one step at a time."

"Exactly. And keep running a visual of your goal a few times a day."

"I have sticky notes to remind me."

"Perfect. Now, even though you feel pressure in your Head Center to know, do you need to know?"

Maggie started to reply and then considered for a moment. "I want to know, but that's when I fall for my mind's strategies. Instead, I'll take a breath and redirect my attention to my Inner Authority. All I need to do is ask. If there is no answer yet, I don't need to know."

"Exactly. You've got this. You just needed a reminder."

"Now, let's look more closely at your chart. Remember your excitement when you realized you wanted to support people in taking charge in their lives?"

Maggie nodded.

"This is in perfect alignment with your life theme or purpose. Look at the Incarnation Cross listed below your chart – LAX Confrontation 1. This is your life purpose, and it's based on the Gates your Conscious and Unconscious Sun and Earth are in. See Gate 45, King/ Queen is at the top of the right-hand column next to the symbol for the Sun. This is the biggest energy in your chart and it's about rulership. Gate 26, The Closer/ Trickster, is below that, next to the Earth sign. It's a powerful sales Gate, and you need to be in integrity with what you're selling. Since your Earth is in this sign, closing deals is grounding for you. Now look at the Unconscious Sun in the left column, in Gate 36, Crisis. This energy is looking for the next new adventure and likes to push to the edge of human experience. However, you need to wait for clarity before jumping into something. Finally, you have your Unconscious Earth in Gate 6, Conflict/ Friction. This powerful energy allows you to penetrate others with ideas, thoughts, or feelings. These four energies combined mean that you can help people take charge, see what's not working, and offer new experiences to help them grow and thrive. Do you see how this aligns perfectly with your soul's desire to help professional women shift their focus to what they love to do?"

"Yes. And based on what you're saying, I am perfectly capable of both selling this concept and leading them to the result."

"Yes. You're fortunate to have the whole Channel 44-26, Surrender. You're uniquely positioned to understand patterns from the past with Gate 44, The Gatherer; glean the lessons; and then bring solutions to your clients that will help them succeed. Furthermore, the planet Pluto is in Gate 44, which means this energy is transformative for you. As you bring solutions based on past patterns to the tribe, you experience transformation personally."

Maggie exhaled. "That eases my fears a bit."

"What are you afraid of?"

"I'm not sure. It's an unknown future, and I've been working in corporations for more than twenty years. This is new territory."

"Yes, and your Gate 57, Intuition, in the Spleen, also has the energy of fear of the future. Since your Conscious Moon is in that Gate, intuition is a powerful driver for you. Let the fear be there and don't buy into it or make it bigger. It's not a signal to stop what you're doing."

"How is my intuition different from my Sacral yes/no responses?"

"How does your intuition inform you?"

Maggie frowned, "It's a knowing. I can't explain it. I just know things."

"Exactly. It's happening so fast that you may be responding to your intuition before you even think to ask yes/no questions. That's okay. I would still bring conscious attention to your yes/no responses and your emotional wave because this is your GPS that can answer your everyday questions. The intuition will also inform and support you."

"Okay. I just feel like I've been on an emotional roller coaster lately, with all my investigations into this new goal."

"Yes, it can be a wild ride. With your Defined Emotional Solar Plexus and Gates 22, Openness, and 30, Passion, you experience a depth of feeling that many don't. This capacity draws people to you, but it also requires awareness to keep from spiraling down into your emotions. Remember how we worked on allowing the feelings but not being taken in by them?"

Maggie nodded.

I continued, "Good. Channel that passion into your work. It's a gift!"

Maggie sighed, "Thanks for that viewpoint. I know we've been over my chart so many times. As I start moving in a new direction in my life, it's taking on new meaning and level of importance. I may be asking you to go through it with me again. I find the information on point."

"Yes, of course. Are there any other questions right now?"

"What is it I need to know that I don't know to ask?"

"That's a great question to give to your intuition. First take some time to come into the witness state accessing Gate 52, Stillness, and you'll get an answer. Your Unconscious Moon is in Gate 52, so when you're rattled, unsure, or overly emotional, you're fortunate to have consistent access to this energy. With this Gate also comes the ability to patiently wait until it's time to take action. Your Open Head will also support you in being quiet. Be sure to set aside time every day to meditate and cultivate your relationship to the stillness."

"Thank you. I feel like I can move forward again."

"Now that you have more experience with using your Human Design strengths and an understanding of how they support your goal, you might listen to the recording of our initial Human Design session where we looked at your chart in detail. See what other strengths you can lean on as you proceed."

Maggie nodded and left smiling to herself.

DECONDITIONING YOUR CENTERS

People with Open Head Centers are more prone to taking on other people's beliefs then people with Defined Head Centers, who tend to know what they think. However, most of our sabotaging beliefs were taken on as young children from parents and teachers, before we were clear on our thoughts. Everyone can benefit from looking at their conditioning and releasing unhelpful beliefs.

Remember, your beliefs determine your experience of reality. For example, if you believe that "life is hard," then the world mirror will reflect that back to you and that will be your experience. Your subconscious is filled with unexamined beliefs that are impacting your current reality.

While writing this book, I've been reading letters between my Mom and Dad written between 1947 and 1949, before their wedding and through the birth of my brother. Mom was worrying about how well things were going and believing that God would surely punish her for some imagined sins and take away the one big thing she wanted – my Dad. As I read this, I remembered that while dating my current partner, I kept waiting for the other shoe to drop. Our relationship was too good to be true, and surely something would take it away. I remember briefly wondering why I felt this way at the time and why it felt so true. The shoe never dropped, but it was a bumpy ride that, in retrospect, could have been smoother!

Let's tune in to beliefs that you're carrying in every Center that are not aligned with the direction you set for yourself and disempower them. Use the life goal you discovered in Chapter 6 and have been visualizing since Chapter 7. Have your Human Design chart handy so you know which Centers are Open or Defined. Start with the following meditation, which is designed to bring up the belief that is currently most detrimental. When that feels complete, go through the full meditation in Appendix D, so you can align each Center to your goal.

MEDITATION TO SURFACE BELIEFS IN THE CENTERS

Close your eyes.

Focus on your breathing as you take three deep slow breaths.

Bring your goal to mind.

Say your goal out loud to yourself.

Your intention is to surface the beliefs that are in the way of your goal.

Ask for support from your higher self to see this.

Inhale deeply, exhale slowly.

With your attention inside yourself, open your eyes, and look at your chart.

Take a deep breath and imagine that this chart is alive inside you.

Locate your Head Center, noting if it's Defined or Open.

Inhale deeply and sense its presence in your head.

Exhale slowly.

Move your attention to the Ajna Center.

Inhale deeply and sense its presence.

Exhale slowly.

Continue with the remaining seven Centers.

Inhaling, sensing its presence, and exhaling slowly.

There is no right way to do this.

Enjoy the experience.

Breathe.

When you're complete, keep your eyes closed.

Relax your breathing and sense the entire bodygraph inside.

Take three deep slow breaths.

Tune in to your goal.

Align with your intention to surface sabotaging beliefs.

Breathe.

Bring to mind a disturbing situation that shows up repeatedly in your life.

Accept whatever situation comes to mind first.

Observe this situation unfolding, as if it's happening now.

Breathe.

Observe without judgment and without resistance.

When you reach the point in this situation where you feel a disturbance or reaction,

direct your attention to where you feel it in the body.

It may show up as an emotion or a pain or other sensation.

Place your full attention on that sensation in your body.

Let go of any resistance to feeling.

Relax your breathing but keep your attention focused in that area.

Let go of thoughts.

Observe the sensation without intensifying it.

Let go of the story of this situation.

Keep returning your attention to the sensation.

Breathe slowly.

If the sensation moves to another part of the body, follow it.

Keep your attention focused on the most intense point of sensation.

Observe.

Breathe slowly.

Memories may surface.

Observe them without attachment.

Keep attention focused on the strongest sensation.

Older memories may surface.
Breathe slowly.
You may feel you're going back in time.
Back to your childhood through this sensation.
All the way back.
Don't think about it.
Breathe.
How old are you and what is happening for you?
Accept whatever impression you get.
What are you as a child, saying to yourself?
Listen.
Maybe you are saying.
They don't listen to me.
They don't like me.
I'm in trouble.
Look at what you as a child are saying.
As you see yourself saying it,
Inhale and hold your breath for as long as you can.
Release.
Let it all go.
Breathe deeply.
You may feel lightness coming in.
You may already feel a release of energy around the situation.
Breathe.
Breathe in self-forgiveness.
Release any judgment on the outbreath.
Breathe in forgiveness of others in this situation.
Breathe out any remnants of that experience.
Feel gratitude for any insights received.
Open your eyes.

Write down a belief you uncovered – what your child was saying. Write down a new one in its place – something you would prefer to experience.

If the old belief surfaces again, it will have less charge or perhaps no charge left. As soon as you see the old belief, stop, take a breath and repeat the new belief to yourself. If you find that the old belief is still highly charged, take it through the Handling Sabotaging Beliefs Process in Appendix E.

Next, go through the full meditation in Appendix D, to focus on each Center and clear conditioning. As part of that process, you'll create a new intention for each Center. You may want to print out a copy of those and post it somewhere you can review it periodically. When you feel it's fully integrated, cross it off the list.

This process will not only surface limiting beliefs, but it will help you recognize goals that you've been conditioned to chase after. After living through World War II and the depression, my parents became very focused on financial goals and encouraged careers that could deliver that. In my early twenties I chased after goals that would give me financial security. While I was successful, my heart felt heavy, and I didn't feel secure. I realized later I was chasing after my parents' goals. They wanted the best for me. It just wasn't in alignment with my true goals. As soon as I started working toward my soul's intention for me, I felt happy and inspired.

SUMMARY

Now that you've cleared some of the patterns, beliefs, and ideas that are not yours, you may be feeling more like your true self. Take a moment to tune into who you are in this moment. Then look at your life goal and say it silently to yourself. Notice if you feel uplifted and inspired. Is this your goal? If *yes*, then proceed. If not, then see how you might adjust it. Perhaps it needs to be bigger or more impactful. Your heart will guide you. Sometimes after releasing parts that are not you, your soul can nudge you toward a dream that perhaps you hadn't dared to claim before – one that seems grand. Listen to that inner guidance. You are grander than that dream. You can do this. Your heart will reward you with happiness.

What's your life dream?

What's your dream as a leader?

It's time to write a new story for yourself.

10

CLAIMING YOUR SOVEREIGNTY AS A LEADER

I t's time to shift the current story of leadership in our world to a broader view. Our world needs different types of leaders to meet people where they are, and to inspire others to show up as the powerful, impactful beings they're designed to be. There are various leadership markers in your chart but claiming your sovereignty by leading your life toward your soul's goal is the highest form of leadership. Your work goals can then be aligned to your life goals. Fully embodying who you are inspires others to do the same and to find their goal. Leaders who are imitating others or trying to please the crowd have vacated themselves and their wisdom. Our world is in need of higher forms of leadership. It needs *your* leadership.

We'll start with a review the rules of the road and get more clarity on working with your attention in service to your goal. Then you'll tune into your leadership style and craft an inspiring intention around it. Let's follow along with Maggie through this experiential review and enjoy the experience.

AN EXPERIENTIAL REVIEW OF THE RULES OF
THE ROAD

Maggie was stuck again.

I was holding space for a breakthrough and started talking in a penetrating voice. "Listen carefully. You have been given tools to work with your wiring, to set a direction, to avoid roadblocks. Yet you're still not creating your preferred reality or realizing your goals. Why not?"

Maggie searched for the right answer, "I'm still giving in to fear? I'm doing it wrong. Wait. I'm not patient enough. Right?"

"Yes. And you may want to investigate the belief that you're 'doing it wrong.' When following your own guidance, it may feel like you're doing it wrong because it's not the same route your mind would take. Listen, don't be hard on yourself. It's common to get tripped up here.

"Let's go over the steps again in a more experiential way. You can close your eyes if you want, but take this in. Let it penetrate your consciousness."

Maggie settled into her cozy chair with a blanket and closed her eyes.

"First you must fully inhabit your vehicle and understand how it works. That's your Human Design. Take a moment to appreciate how perfectly you're designed. What you call 'weaknesses' are not that. They are part of your design. You have so many strengths to lean on. Settle into your design and fully inhabit it.

"You've been working with your Human Design over these past several months, and that's working for you now. So, notice what happens when fear is triggered. You're no longer inhabiting your vehicle but instead hovering nearby. Can you feel that?"

Maggie nodded with her eyes closed.

"From there, you can't work the steering wheel. You can't actually drive your vehicle if you're not in it.

"Second step: decide on your destination.

"You can't lead if you don't know where you're headed. You can't drive the car if you don't know your destination. That's clear. Right?"

Maggie nodded again.

"Third: control your attention. Stay awake.

"Every time you fall asleep, your vehicle is being driven by something or someone else, not by you. Either the circumstances in the environment around you are in control or, worse, someone else with their own agenda is in control.

"Stay awake. There are more dangers. Control your attention.

"Every time you react negatively to bumps in the road, you're detouring off the route and will encounter more problems. The mirror will oblige your request for more negativity, and you'll continue to move away from your desired destination.

"Wake up. Control your attention. See the bumps as part of your path, nothing more. Stay aware.

"Now, take your hands off the steering wheel.

"Visualize your destination and let nature or your inner guidance navigate for you. Nature is highly efficient. It never wastes energy and so it will take you the optimal route. Your brain can't possibly do that.

"Wake up. Control your attention.

"See the advantage or silver lining in every speed bump, and you won't detour off the highway into a rat's maze. If you react negatively, remember what you get – more speedbumps. Laugh when you hit a bump and focus on the solution. Don't focus on the problem. You can't change the present or the past, but you can move toward a different future.

"Wake up. Control your attention.

"Let go of the steering wheel and keep the goal in mind without exerting effort. Using effort means you don't believe you'll get there. Remember, you are choosing off a menu of destinations and the GPS will take you there. Don't worry. Be patient. Let go.

"Wake up. Control your attention.

"Now enjoy the scenery, fall in love with the journey, with yourself, with nature. Allow yourself to feel the joy that naturally occurs as your move along your path.

"Embody the version of you that has already reached the goal. Act and talk like them.

"Don't grab that steering wheel.

"Nature is taking you on the optimal route. Don't let your mind grab the wheel.

"Wake up. Control your attention.

"Listen for the next action step to take. It will be given to you.

"Ask yes/no questions if you have a Defined Sacral and you'll get answers.

"Otherwise, tune in to your guidance or talk out loud so you can hear yourself.

"Get clear on your next step.

"Now take the step. Visualization without action is useless.

"Wake up. Control your attention.

"Surrender your personal motives to your inner guidance. Allow yourself to be led step by step if you don't want major detours.

"Wake up. Surrender. Commit to following your guidance.

"By allowing yourself to be led in this way, you are in fact leading yourself by using the power and wisdom of your higher self.

"Wake up.

"Observe.

"Listen.

"Follow.

"When you are awake and aware, seeing reality as it is, your inner guidance will nudge you into right action. If no guidance is coming, visualize your goal and ask again.

"Wake up. Control your attention.

"Controlling attention is vital to creating your reality. You have two major levers – attention and intention."

After a few moments, Maggie opened her eyes excitedly. "Wow. I get it on a deeper level. Thank you. I am leading myself. I'm sovereign."

Then she thought for a moment. "Can you say more about controlling my attention? I understand about avoiding negativity and focusing on the solution... Oh, on the future. Is that what you mean?"

"Exactly. Great observation. You can't change the present. You have to accept it and set your goal for the future. Now, since you asked about attention, let's go a little deeper into how to direct your attention."

DIRECTING YOUR ATTENTION

"First, place all of your attention out on the room. Do you notice what your eyes are doing?"

Maggie thought for a moment. "They're scanning the room and focusing here and there."

"Perfect. Your awareness is growing tremendously. Could you feel that when you were scanning the room, you vacated yourself? You've disconnected from your inner guidance and have no idea what is going on inside."

"Give me a minute. Okay. That's true," she said slowly.

"Now focus all of your attention inward. Keep the eyes open, but all your attention is inside so you're not really looking out of your eyes. Even though your eyes are open you're not really seeing what is going on around you.

"What do you notice?"

"I can feel my anxiousness."

"Great. Do you have any idea what is happening out here?"

"No."

"All right, now focus on both your internal and external environments at the same time.

"Can you tell me what's happening with your eyes?"

"They're relaxed. Not focused at all."

"Yes. You can only do this from a relaxed place. Now you can feel what is happening inside at the same time you can observe what is happening around you."

"Yes, I can. Why is that important?"

"This allows you to respond appropriately to whatever is happening. You have access to your guidance, so if something arises unexpectedly, you can handle it. If you're talking with someone, you can keep your attention on them and listen to them, and at the same time your attention is inside tuning in to your guidance. You'll feel more connected to the other person, and they will feel heard. Your guidance will provide you with the most appropriate response. You'll say whatever the person needs to hear."

"That would be amazing. Whoops, it feels harder to focus my attention in both places when I'm the one speaking."

"Rather than focusing your attention, widen it back; relax and allow yourself to see both inside and out. With practice, this gets easier. For you, it's especially powerful; you have Channel 57-20, The Brainwave, which connects Gate 57, Intuition, from the Spleen to Gate 20, In the Now, coming off the Throat. You have consistent access to your intuition as you're speaking in the moment. If you find your eyes, tensing up, it's a clue that you're overly focused on the external environment and disconnecting from your inner genius."

"I like that – inner genius. When you say to wake up and control my attention, then I should make sure I'm relaxed and placing attention on my inner and outer worlds at the same time."

"Yes. The relaxation will happen naturally as you direct your attention in this way. After you've practiced this for a while, we'll add some steps to your visualization practice to make it more powerful. Now you can take some time to celebrate your sovereignty as a leader. You're able to take full responsibility for creating your reality, for understanding your design, for leading your life by setting a direction and moving toward it. Congratulations!

CREATING A NEW LEADERSHIP STORY

"Thank you! But there is more to being a leader than that."

"What more is there?"

"A leader is someone who inspires others and guides them toward a common goal. A leader is decisive and confident and wise and compassionate and has vision."

"Wait a minute. Leaders do have a wide-ranging set of qualities and attributes, but the most effective ones have something in common."

"What is that?"

"They lead based on their strengths, by fully embodying their design. This naturally inspires others to align."

"Yes, I know, and setting a direction and moving toward it. But my company always rated our leadership on certain attributes they valued in their leaders such as being hardworking, and having confidence, decisiveness and empathy. And although I was highly productive, they thought I was a little slow on making decisions. I know now to wait out my emotional wave, but at the time, all I knew was that I wasn't clear. It was frustrating. I never received high marks there."

"What happened when you made decisions quickly?"

"I usually paid for it. I signed a contract once without running it by the CFO. I was under pressure, and everyone else was fine with it. I got into big trouble there. We missed a clause in the contract that the Finance Department was not happy about. I can think of a couple of other bad decisions."

"See what happens when there is too much emphasis on certain traits like making decisions quickly? Taking enough time to decide is not a weakness; it's your design. Navigate according to your design and your power will shine through."

Maggie nodded deep in thought.

I continued. "And if your leadership style and strengths are different from what's valued in your company, you're still better off being who you are. Trying to imitate someone else doesn't inspire anyone. Your heart will never align with that goal. If you try to do that, your mind will take over and you'll lose connection to your guidance. You will no longer be following you. Other people will not be inspired to follow you either."

"True. It's obvious when a manager tries to be someone they're not. No one wants to work for them."

"It's time for you to write a new leadership story and honor your ability to take charge, learn from old patterns, and bring change that allows people to grow and thrive. Take some time to write out an intention for your style of leadership, something that inspires you – your credo that you can live by. Find that place of stillness inside and see what comes to you.

I'd love to. Thank you."

LEADERSHIP STYLES

As Maggie left, I marveled once again at the variety of leadership styles in my clients and their success stories. When someone understands their Human Design, they also understand why they lead and how they lead best. This is more important than trying to live up to a specific set of leadership traits. Many companies are more sophisticated in their evaluation of leaders. Instead of highlighting specific leadership qualities, they look at your natural strengths to learn why you lead the way you do and how you lead most effectively. For example, you might have an influencing style and like to present information to groups from the front of the room. Manifesting Generators, like Maggie, would excel at this with their motor to the Throat. Perhaps your style is more like an achiever or motivator, and you like to galvanize teams to reach stretch goals. Most likely this type of leader has a Defined Will Center who can push others and perhaps a Defined Identity Center where they know where they're headed and expect others to follow. Perhaps your style is a relationship builder where you listen to everyone's story, see the unique talents they bring, and leverage those. Jackie is this type of leader. Let's look at her style along with some of the other leaders we've already introduced.

Jackie is a Generator (see Chart C) and has a natural ability to make people feel at ease, so they open up to her. She responds to her team members and coworkers in a professional yet nurturing way. She has Channel 27-50, Preservation, which is also nicknamed the Mother Theresa Channel. She must be careful not to give too much and exhaust herself, but she has the gift of teaching values and caring for the group. She is also clear on everyone's strengths and how to best use them. Sensing her openness, even her boss confides in her and seeks her input.

You may remember Patty from Chapter 5. As a Projector (refer to Chart F), she's a wise guide and supports leaders in unusual ways. She's here to challenge conventional wisdom and find a higher way. You might label her leadership style as strategic thinker – one who likes to brainstorm to find better solutions for the business. However, her style requires a more nontraditional leadership descriptor. Patty uses storytelling to make her radical ideas more accessible to those who might otherwise be skeptical or afraid. She weaves in lessons from the past to support her solutions that help others thrive. Perhaps we could call her leadership style a "crazy wisdom teacher."

Sarah, a Manifestor (see Chart E), is here to impact people in a big way with her breakthrough insights that benefit everyone. People seek out her wisdom and find themselves telling her their deepest desires and secrets. With Channel 43-23, Structuring or Insight, she can see what new knowledge is worthy of pursuing and assimilating into the world. She has a deep passion for life with Gate 30, Passion. She's looking for new experiences and has many different talents with Channel 36-35, Transitoriness. As a Manifestor, she is here to lead by initiating and impacting people and situations. She acts independently, is self-possessed, and exudes capability. As a 6/2 Profile, she is a wise guide with innate gifts to offer the world. With this abundance of leadership gifts, Sarah's style is hard to label, but it would likely include Innovative Influencer.

Barbara, a Reflector (see Chart G), is here to disseminate knowledge to those who are ready to learn from her. She's mirroring back to us the health of our community and offering her guidance there. She is also reflecting the parts of us that are normally hidden. It takes courage to fully align with her, but it's worth it. Her leadership style is one of assessing without judgment and offering a suggested way forward.

Can you see how important it is to understand and appreciate the many varied textures of leadership – how it enriches all our lives? Leadership is about understanding, accepting, and embodying who you are. This inspires others to be their authentic selves as well.

Your Human Design can give you deep insights into your

natural style of leadership. In working with your chart, you can discover and lean on your strengths. You have information on how you influence others, how you analyze or deal with information and situations, and how you nurture relationships. Perhaps most importantly, through your Type, Strategy, and Authority, you can rely on your decision-making and communicate effectively, so you can succeed in life. Take a moment to tune into your style of leadership. What does your highest form of leadership look like? Is this inspiring to you? If not, tune in to your guidance. What do you need to fan that spark inside so you can shine your brilliance in all aspects of your life? Write it down. Craft a statement that is inspiring to you. This is your new story of leadership; your leadership credo. Lead from there!

Our world needs your brand of leadership.

11

ENGAGING OTHERS WITH DIFFERENT DESIGNS

How might you support others more effectively now that you've learned some basics around Human Design and leading your life? By now you may appreciate the variety of ways people interface with the world and make decisions. To inspire and motivate people, you not only have to embody your own form of leadership, but you also need to observe other people's behaviors and engage in conversations to understand their way of leading. Become curious. Observing, listening, and communicating without judgment can help build successful relationships. You can always rely on your Type, Strategy, and Authority for support. Let's start with Maggie's concerns around this.

Maggie was back in my office again with more questions.

"This has been all about me and leading my life. What about working with other people? I have a new appreciation for how differently everyone is wired. How do I deal with a team member who doesn't follow through? I can't seem to motivate him. I can't relate because I've always followed through."

"Your team member most likely has an Open Will Center,

since only one-eighth of the population has this Center Defined and usually does what they say they're going to do. Many people with an Open Will Center attend motivational events with speakers like Tony Robbins to improve themselves in some area of life. They get fired up and go home with every intention of following through on their commitments, and then they don't. Then they might beat themselves up and the cycle starts over again. They likely don't realize they have an Open Will Center and are not designed to just do it. Instead, they're here to explore what they value and to become wise about it. Deep down, they may value connection or making a creative contribution over finishing a project. Furthermore, these people may not have thought about what they value – especially the ones attending motivational events. You have to link the project they're working on to something they value. Have a conversation with them where you explore what is important to them and explain how this project is aligned with that. This exploration will support your team member because they likely have some conditioning to clear in that Center. They may have taken on their parent's values and never examined them. Or they may be questioning their value and need support in this area. Listen to what they have to say. Check your Inner Authority by asking yourself yes/no questions for the correct timing and approach.

"That's a helpful perspective and I look forward to some interesting conversations. Can you say more about what else I might encounter in working with others? I'm trying to understand how to use this information to support my team."

"You may not know your team members' designs, but you can observe how people interact and respond accordingly. You can start with the premise that they're doing the best they can with their design. This way you don't see the other person as wrong or needing to be "fixed". Self-development is always recommended and should be encouraged, but simply assuming that something is wrong with them is not a good starting point. When you're seeing them through that lens, your decisions will be biased, and they'll likely feel unacknowledged, unseen, and unappreciated. It's important for you to be observant and notice when you are aligning with unhelpful beliefs. Then use the process we've practiced for releasing it. As you work with others, you continue to work on yourself."

"Okay, I'm beginning to get more clarity on my attitude in dealing with others. Can you say more about what to observe in them and how I might bring out their best?"

"Great question. Let's look at what you know so far about Human Design and see what you might infer about others. For example, if someone is speaking and no one is listening, ask them a question so they can be in response. Remember from our work together that only Manifestors can effectively initiate without needing to be in response, and that they are 8 percent of the population. They tend to work alone or in leadership positions. It's unlikely you'll have one of them on your team. Ninety-two percent of us have a Strategy that includes being in response. Manifesting Generators can also initiate after they receive an internal *yes* or in response to something from outside of them.

"Team members with Defined Head and Ajna Centers are broadcasting ideas and tend to express their ideas from a place of certainty. They're not always right, so be sure to ask clarifying questions. Those with Open Head Centers are taking in ideas and trying them on. They're generally not certain or may not remember details, but their input is valuable too. They can usually remember an impression of something, so don't press them for details. Give everyone an opportunity to be in response. Invite them to speak. If someone is not participating in a discussion, ask their viewpoint. They might be a Projector or someone with an Open Throat Center.

"If you know one of your team members has trouble starting projects, and they work from home, you can get more creative. They may have an Open Root. Since roughly half of the population has a Defined Root, they can pair up with someone to get access to that energy. Suggest that they get on Zoom with another team member, not to talk, but to have a line of connection open while they're working. In the presence of the other person, they may have access to that starting energy and will be more productive. This same approach works well with people who have trouble competing projects.

"If someone doesn't seem to have energy for long days at work, they may have an Open Sacral Center. Perhaps they can get a lot done in a short time, but their energy wanes in the afternoon. See if you can be more flexible with their office hours, or at least let them take a break sometime where they can be alone and rest. Focus more on their output than on the hours they work. Otherwise, they may burn out or become sick. Generators and Manifesting Generators can burnout too if they are working on projects for which they have a *no*. Be observant about people's skill sets and do your best to assign projects that make use of each one's skills. If they need to complete a project that you believe they have a *no* for, then work with them to see if you can make it more appealing to them or assign it to someone else. Aligning their tremendous capacity to work with what they like to do will pay off in productivity. It's worth a little time and effort.

"Some people thrive on more extreme schedules – working for three days straight and then resting for a couple of days. You'd probably recognize it if someone on your team works like this. How can you accommodate them? These Types don't often work in companies unless they're conditioned to believe they should work 9:00 a.m. to 5:00 p.m. If they're on your team, see how you can honor their schedule and focus on their results.

"Some people are sensitive to their environment and need the freedom to setup their workspace in a way that makes them feel good. They may have an Open G Center or Gate 19, Sensitivity. Some workers keep themselves busy in order to try to relieve the pressure they feel from their Open Root. This not only creates extra work – not only for themselves, but also possibly for other team members too – and it doesn't relieve their pressure. They can be supported to allow the pressure and discern what actually needs to be done.

"Some people are designed to work in collaboration, and others do better on their own. If someone is perceived as not being a team player, well, you're familiar with that scenario."

Maggie smiled. "I'm beginning to see where bringing in a Human Design consultant could be effective."

"Yes. For now, work from what you already know. At this point in your journey, you know more than you realize. Understanding there are different ways of working and decision-making, and allowing for that, is a big step toward supporting people to be themselves and to flourish. Too often we think that others' low energy or their inability to remember things are weaknesses that need to be improved. Instead, we need to focus on the underlying issue, put strategies into place where needed and then help them to build their strengths. Those perceived 'weaknesses' are likely part of their design. They may be pain points, but through awareness and exploration, they can become wisdom Centers. Then everyone benefits. Team members can be supported to contribute without having to compromise who they truly are.

"As you claim your sovereignty and show up as unapologetically you, permission is given for others to show up this way. When you allow the other to be who they are, both of you experience more freedom. Finding a way to do this effectively is a skill you'll master over time. Stay aware and curious and... "

Maggie joined in, "Follow my Type, Strategy, and Author-ity. It always comes down to that, doesn't it? I have the answers inside, and when I need more information, I know where to look. Once again, I am feeling more sovereign. Thank you."

"Enjoy the journey! Remember, my door is always open."

EXTRA COMMUNICATION AND TOLERANCE REQUIRED

Sometimes it can be challenging to operate within the rules of a work environment while still honoring your design. While some employers are willing to adjust their workplaces to fit the needs of different workers, others are still too rigid, and they lose talented employees. I believe that some of this rigidity stems from misunderstanding and lack of communica-tion. For example, people with several Defined Centers in their design don't realize how differently people with several Open Centers operate and respond to situations and environ-ments. They may set unrealistic expectations for them. With just a bare-bones understanding of Human Design, you prob-ably already have more appreciation for the variety of styles, and you know some questions to ask to open up dialogue. Let's look at a couple of stories here that highlight potential workplace and relationship issues.

Theresa is an emotional Generator (see Chart J in the Appendix) with extreme rhythms. She's highly creative and can produce more work in a few hours than most people produce in a week, as she possesses the time-bender Channel 44-26, Surrender. Once she starts on a project, she works late into the night or sometimes overnight to complete it (having Gate 15, Extremes). Then she needs rest. Recently she started working for a young company to setup its training depart-ment. She worked tirelessly for the first couple of weeks in her home studio to put together a set of professional training videos. The company managers were excited about her work. However, despite the fact that she worked all weekend, her boss still expected her to be at her office desk from eight to five on weekdays. Though Theresa is more productive at home and in the late-night hours, she tried to conform to her boss's rule of regular, in-person work hours. One day, Theresa asked to work remotely for a couple of days so she could visit with her daughter, and her boss said no. Theresa, exhausted from working extreme hours and working business hours, pushed back. She almost left the company, until upper management listened to her concerns and were willing to accommodate her schedule.

Theresa did the work of three people and produced effective training videos with no budget other than her salary. Other companies of the same size have significant advertising budgets for this activity. Yet she was criticized for her work habits. Fortunately, we had gone over her design before she took the job, so she understood what she needed to perform well in a work environment. This gave her courage to speak to upper management and effect change. They didn't want to lose her talent. Eventually, she did leave because middle management couldn't tolerate a separate work rule for Theresa.

Quality relationships are at the core of business and personal success and fulfillment. Understanding who you are can inspire more productive communication, not just at the office, but also at home.

Hannah (see Chart K in the Appendix) came to me with a relationship issue. She is an emotional Generator with seven Defined Centers and a Triple Split Definition. Her last partner was dependent on her and came across as very needy at times. Hannah felt stifled and eventually ended the relationship. Now she was dating someone new. While she felt love for him, she didn't feel that she "needed" him and wondered about it. Was this relationship right for her?

With seven Defined Centers, Hannah tended to be solid in herself and not so easily influenced. She was somewhat familiar with Human Design and thought perhaps that Gate 63, Doubt, was to blame. I explained that while she could be misusing that Gate of Doubt and turning it on herself, I believed something else was at play. With her Triple Split Definition, where her Centers were in three groupings, no one person could complete her. If they did, she might feel stifled or trapped in the relationship. Referring to her chart, you'll see the Centers in three groups: the Ajna and Throat Centers; the G, Sacral, and Emotional Solar Plexus Centers; and the Root and Spleen Centers. This is a transpersonal design. She gets her flow from being out in public and by nature, she is independent and whole within herself.

This doesn't mean Hannah can't be in relationships, but rather that she doesn't "need" that relationship to complete her. Her previous partner may have experienced wholeness with her because she may have bridged a Small Split for him. Remember from Chapter 4 that people with a Small Split are electromagnetically looking for someone with the corresponding Gate to close the gap. Hannah can have a beautiful relationship with someone who is comfortable with her independence. My partner has a Triple Split Definition and mine is Single (all my Centers connect), so both of us are independent and still we have an extraordinary connection and a close, enduring partnership.

Hannah was relieved to hear this. When she let go of the expectation that her relationship would bring her some imagined need to feel whole or complete, the relationship deepened. She began to go to a local coffee shop in the mornings to get her flow going and then come home to her partner, free of expectation.

It may seem daunting to understand and leverage your design as well as trying to decipher other people's designs. Perhaps you can begin to see that it comes down to being curious about others and observing how they operate. Communicating frequently with others, and listening to their viewpoints without judgment, goes a long way toward building successful relationships. Tuning in to your Type, Strategy, and Authority about what to say and when to say it is your greatest tool. The answers are there for you, and if you're not receiving guidance, be patient. The answers will come.

THE JOURNEY FORWARD

WHAT YOU'RE TAKING WITH YOU

Now it's time for you to move forward in your life with the insights you've gleaned from our work so far. You've received a lot of information to assimilate, yet you've just scratched the surface of this rich and complex modality that is Human Design. Nonetheless you've persevered through to this point, working with you Type, Strategy, and Authority – the fundamental underpinning of the chart.

We've covered a lot of ground in this book to support you in becoming a more effective leader. After looking at your Type, Strategy, and Authority, you learned about the world mirror and how you receive whatever you present to it. Then we looked at your story of leadership, based on your current reality, without judgment. Anything you're resisting from your current experience follows you to the preferred reality you're creating. This gave you incentive to face and handle triggers from your current world.

Then you set a direction. Sometimes it's easier to know

what you don't want than what you do want. Until now your mind has put so many limitations on you that you might have felt like your heart was in a cage. You started listening more deeply to your heart by looking at your soul's goal for you, free of constraints. That sparked a desire in you to move toward it. You visualized the new reality, with the idea that it's already created. All versions of reality exist in this vast universe somewhere in the form of information. By aligning with the *you* that already created it, and adopting the attitudes and habits of this new one, you're propelled along a life path toward your dream goal.

There are usually roadblocks and challenges along the way. You investigated some of the universal blocks such as guilt and inferiority. Then you shifted from viewing them as obstacles to seeing them as part of your path. You looked more deeply at the Openness and Definition in your Centers. Since conditioning more readily lands in the Open Centers, you surfaced some sabotaging beliefs related to your intention. You had an opportunity to examine these beliefs, release them and create new ones.

Then you worked on controlling your attention. There are two levers available to you for creating your reality – intention and attention. You learned the importance of directing your attention both inside and outside at the same time. You're well-equipped to move farther along toward your goal.

You also received some insights into how others work and hopefully an appreciation for the differences among people's approaches. Through your current understanding of Human Design and how you operate you could observe others and better determine what support they need. Ideally you could create Human Design charts for them, but even with your current knowledge, you can already observe and have fruitful conversations with them.

Above all, you've written a new story of leadership and

claimed your sovereignty. You understand the value of allowing others to be themselves and they're inspired by the way you are unapologetically *you*.

You've successfully completed the Lead by Design training, and you may be wondering what's next. Do you want support with integrating this into your life or with going deeper in the materials? Do you want support with your teams at work? Is there something else you need? You decide.

GUIDANCE FOR YOUR JOURNEY

As you move forward with this process, you may want support to become more skillful with navigating your particular life path, like Maggie did. Honor that desire for support if it arises, especially if you don't want to spend a lot of time and effort learning Human Design. Given the complexity of the Human Design system, I was lucky to have Robin as a teacher to help me embody this work. If you want to go deeper into the Human Design aspects of your chart, there are many ways to do that, and we can have a conversation about it. It's become a popular topic in recent years, and there is a proliferation of materials and ideologies about it. My lineage for this piece of our work together is through Robin, who learned from her teacher, Karen Curry Parker, who learned from Ra, who received the original transmission.

Taking what you learn from Human Design and applying it to consciously leading your life is the journey we've begun here. There is much more to learn. As you gain experience with what you already know, you'll start to see how creatively the Universe is supporting you in helping you achieve your goals. The power you now wield is beyond anything you can imagine. The Catch-22 is that it takes humility to wield it. You're leading by allowing yourself to be led by your inner guidance.

It's easy to get off track and go down a rabbit hole of discouragement or, conversely, go off on a power trip. These sidesteps all lead to the same mess – major detours off your route. Recognize that you are creating your reality. Where do you want to go? You now know the most efficient route to get there. Remember that the energy field and habits of the old *you* may still have a strong gravitational pull. It requires consistent practice to escape that field and to propel yourself into a new space in which the new you has already created your soul's desire. The world mirror has a built-in delay. In that delay, you may forget and lose your way or change direction because you believe that "This one isn't working." Someone who can see the bigger picture and remind you of the progress you're making can help you avoid those detours.

I find this happens frequently with clients. There is a period in which they're dedicated and making progress. Then they hit a challenge and start believing their mind's assessments and start following the path it presents. They're on a huge detour route before they realize it and they need support to get back on track, following their soul's path.

Stay aware and refuse to align with negativity, guilt, inferiority, seriousness, and not allowing yourself to "have". Remember that guilt is insidious and creeps in in the most unexpected ways. Stay awake. Opportunities to feel inferior and superior abound because your mind is a measurement tool and is constantly comparing. Beware or be aware. You can be serious about the commitment to your path and your practices; however, when you make the goal too serious, or your actions come from a place of "importance," your goal moves further from you. Seriousness shuts down access to your frontal lobe where higher functions such as compassion exist. Making something too important creates an imbalance in energies and nature will knock it off the pedestal. Holding your journey, goal, and process lightly is critical for success.

Be serious about your commitment, but meet life –especially your challenges –with lightness.

Not allowing yourself to "have" is an obstacle learned from early childhood. "You can't have that toy. Put it back. No, you can't have ice cream before dinner. No, you can't follow your dream. Be realistic." As an adult you might find yourself peering into shop windows wishing you could afford those designer clothes or driving past Lexus dealerships dreaming. "No, I can't have a luxury car. I don't dare go for a test drive. They'll know I'm a fraud." Retraining yourself to "have", can be quite an amusing journey when you encounter this issue. It's one of my favorite trainings. It starts with debunking the myth that just because you have something doesn't mean you're depriving someone else of it. Everyone is responsible for their experience of reality.

I've been blessed with a great deal of support in my life, through of a series of spiritual and professional mentors who showed up before I knew I needed them. Without their transmissions, I would be living an entirely different life. I'd be leading someone else's idea for me. A mentor or someone who has "been there" and knows a way through can hold the highest vision for you, even when you can't yet claim it for yourself. We're not meant to be loners. Most of us are explicitly designed to be relational beings and almost all of us are designed to live in society and interact with other people. A guide willing to walk alongside you can be invaluable.

GUIDANCE FOR YOUR TEAM OR FAMILY

Maybe you'd like support with bringing Human Design and these leadership principles to your team or business. Most people love to learn more about themselves and others, especially when the learnings are easily obtained from their birth information. How would it be to have your whole team engaged in fruitful conversations about the best way to communicate with each other and make decisions? What rules might make sense in your workplace to accommodate the different designs?

Perhaps you'd like to bring this closer to home and get a handle on how to communicate better with your partner or rejuvenate the relationship. Lucy came to me before heading out for a weekend bachelorette party in Vegas with friends. She had almost decided not to go because she ends up feeling alone and disconnected. Lucy has a 5/1 learning Profile where she is here to save the world through practical solutions that help people. A consequence of this Profile is that people project on her in both negative and positive ways, because they sense that she can help them. On top of this she has seven Open Centers and many patterns of trauma in them.

With her Open Throat Center, she needed to be asked her opinion before speaking. Upon hearing this, Lucy felt an odd sense of relief, especially around the projections. They weren't personal and she couldn't do anything about them anyway. She committed to following her Strategy to respond and to following her Sacral Authority. She had a fantastic weekend. Lucy was able to hold herself back from blurting out her opinions, and she realized what a mess that could have been. Because she only spoke in response, she felt heard and acknowledged. She also felt accepted and connected with this group in a way she had never experienced before. Relationships can be healed even if only one person does this work. It's more fun and more powerful when two or more become involved with it.

When you're ready, there's much more to discover about yourself and those you lead and loved ones in your life. I look forward to sharing more layers of this work when the timing is right for you.

A NOTE ABOUT BIRTH INFORMATION

If you have your birth date but not the specific time of your birth, we can still find your chart. This involves asking you specific questions that help us discern your likely birth time. Also, occasionally the birth time that was originally recorded may not be exactly correct. You may remember my response to Yolanda's chart in Chapter 2. If there's reason to believe that the recorded birth time is not quite right, we can check that as well.

IN SUMMARY

The potential obstacles are many and the information is deep and wide. Sometimes it's like standing at the mouth of a gushing river and trying to take a drink. It's helpful if someone hands you cup.

Take your time drinking it all in.

Trust your process.

LEAD BY DESIGN

Human Design applied to leadership principles, can change your experience of life at work and at home. Leading from a solid sense of who you are, while developing your skills in the Lead by Design process, is fulfilling and effective. It's a solid foundation from which to reach toward your inspired goals. The impact of embodying all aspects of you can't be underestimated. Others will feel that sense of harmony and wholeness around you. The world mirror amplifies this, and so more people will be attracted to you.

Human Design gives people permission to be themselves, and this is the most common feedback I hear. People start to internalize the idea that they don't have "weaknesses" so much as design differences from those of other people. Self-acceptance is one of the desired leadership traits. You can always create strategies for handling Human Design traits that seem to get in the way. Don't try to change who you are. This is where people get into trouble.

Can you see the possibilities in your design and how aligning with it can make you a strong leader? Can you feel the power of claiming your sovereignty regardless of the cultural norms? Do you see how doing so inspires others to show up as their best selves, contributing to society in a big way?

Human Design is that missing link that gives us deep insight into how others operate. I loved Myers Briggs and the DISC assessments when they came out. I studied Enneagram for a while and tried to apply it to my family relationships. I was so thirsty for information on how different people operated so I could relate better. While each of these modalities offer a great step forward, most of them depend on questionnaires. While people may answer with the best of intentions, they're usually giving conditioned responses without realizing it. As soon as I looked at Human Design, I was surprised – how could birth date, time, and city reveal so much?

Then I remembered my trainings in India – most of our life script is written before and during the birth process. Conditioning starts at conception. The energies impacting us in the womb and at birth are imprinting gifts, challenges, and conundrums. It's all in your chart from the very beginning.

I wish I had known Human Design concepts when I was training Debra to run workshops. She would show up just before we started, no matter how often I asked her to help with setup. She would sleep at lunch instead of helping us prepare for the balance of the day. Imagine that! I labeled her a Diva; yet I still continued to work with her because during the training sessions themselves, our partnership was magical. She had tremendous potential. I realized I was dealing with my belief that I shouldn't have to be the one to do all the setup work. Now I know that by design, she is a Projector and needs rest. That information would have been useful when we were working together. I was trying to train her to do all parts of a weekend course– enrolling, setup, facilitation, clean up. I could have let go of my preconceived notions and found another way. Instead, I set up and cleaned up with frustration. After all, Debra was twenty years younger than me, so she "should" have had more energy.

This is what we do to each other – set expectations based on our experience and when the person falls short, we blame them. "Work on your weak spots. Here they are!" Why should this person have the same level of energy as you? Should they follow through on everything they say? What if you inquired without judgment about what was going on for them? Too many Projectors I know have hit burnout multiple times in their lives because they were trying to be Generators. Too many Generators have also hit burnout because they were not following their inner *noes*. Understanding each other's differences can lead to a profound sense of compassion, and a deep realization that we're all in this together.

You're now well-equipped to lead purposely and from your strengths. How do you feel about where you stand in relationship to leading right now?

Do you feel more empowered to step more fully into your leadership role? Do you have lingering questions with which you might want support?

Take a moment to stand in the truth of who you are and claim your sovereignty. There is no one else like you. Your unique style of leadership is a gift that powerfully impacts those around you. Reread your new leadership story, your personal credo. Anchor those in.

From this place enjoy the following experiential meditation that reviews the Lead by Design concepts around leading your life in alignment with your soul's goal. Find a comfortable place to lie down and relax into this experience. Allow it to sink into your consciousness – as a reminder of your magnificence.

Remember you are the Center of the Universe.

No more playing small.

Stay awake and aware.

EXPERIENTIAL REVIEW OF THE LEAD BY DESIGN CONCEPTS

You Are the Center of the Universe Meditation

Feel free to lie down with a blanket and pillow for this meditation.
Close your eyes and slow down your breathing.
Take in a deep full breath.
Exhale slowly.
Release anything you are holding on the outbreath.
Continue breathing slow and deep.
Feel your body resting on the Earth.
Feel the support underneath you.
Let go.
Let your body get heavy.
Feel your body become so heavy that you seem to lift right out of it.
Let yourself rise up and out.
Floating freely in the atmosphere.
Breathe.
Rise up and out into the galaxy.
Looking back at the Earth - so beautiful, so blue.
As you look around at the stars and planets, this space seems so vast.
Infinite space.
Beyond your ability to grasp.
Let go and allow yourself to be held in the vastness of the Universe.
Infinity means the Center is everywhere.
You are the Center.
Take that in as you float in space.
You are the Center of this Universe.
The Center of the Universe is located everywhere.
Everything that has ever been created or will be created is here now.

The Center is in every point.

Every point at the same time.

All events exist concurrently.

Past, present, and future are all here now.

Everything is emerging in the moment.

Everything is alive.

You are creating your life this very moment.

You're only keeping the past alive by replaying it.

It's using your energy to stay alive.

See your energy keeping the past alive.

Let it go.

The future is also alive.

The future has infinite variations.

All versions of the future exist in the information space.

Somewhere out there in the vast Universe,

your future is constantly emerging, shifting, and reorganizing.

It's influencing your current life path.

Your future responds to your thoughts, words and actions.

Be clear in your intentions.

The future is responding.

All your intentions are already created right now.

They exist in the information field.

Which version of the future will you choose?

Or will you let others choose for you?

Stay awake.

Be aware.

One version of your future is present on your current trajectory.

Choose your future wisely.

Listen to your soul's intention for you.

Hold your intention lightly and with resoluteness, knowing it's already done.

Feel that solidity of knowing it's done.

Stay awake.

Be present.

The you that created this intention is here now.
Be that person now.
Embody them.
Feel how it is to be that version of you.
Adopt the attitude.
Adopt the habits.
Take action aligned with this new version of you.
Trust. Be patient.
Stay awake. Be present.
Everything is emerging in the moment.
Here now.
Keep holding to your intention without desire, without making it important.
Allow yourself to have
Let go of guilt and inferiority, knowing that if you don't let it go, your future path will shift to include more of that.
Visualize your intention.
Allow yourself to have.
Stay awake.
Be present.
Keep holding to the vision without want or need but simply knowing it's done.
Walk around in your vision.
See through the eyes of the one in the vision.
You are the participant here, not the observer.
Everything is emerging in the moment.
Breathe up and down your spine increasing the energy.
Stay awake.
Be present.
Release the vision.
Trust.
Don't allow yourself to indulge in negative thoughts, or the world mirror will reflect more negativity.
Stay awake.

Be present.

Where is your attention right now?

The Universe is arranging events to bring you opportunities.

Nature operates in the most efficient way.

It doesn't waste energy.

It's bringing you what you are visualizing and embodying.

Stay awake and aware.

Be present.

Watch your thoughts.

When you notice any small sign that your intention is creating, celebrate.

Nurture that joy.

The world mirror will reflect more of that back to you.

Stay awake and aware.

Respond appropriately in the moment.

When your guidance says to take a step, do it.

When your mind tells you to act, stop.

This is new territory.

Only your inner guidance knows the way.

Stay awake and aware.

Be present.

Where are your directing your intention?

Listen to that still small voice guiding you every step of the way.

Stay awake and aware.

Be present.

Don't reach and grasp for the goal.

Know that it's created.

It's here now.

You are that person now.

Embody that one.

The one that already created it.

Stay awake and aware.

Breathe.

Your old self is tugging at you, trying to pull you back.

Remember how comfortable it was to play small?
To shut out the world or to distract with busyness
Your mind has many reasons to stay comfortable.
Beware.
Let go.
Nurture the joy of having what you intend.
Nurture the joy of being what you intend.
What you desire is your soul's desire.
Allow yourself to have.
Allow yourself to have.
It's a choice.
Everyone can have what they desire.
No limits.
Allow yourself to have your soul's desire.
Feel the joy of creating this.
Be that joy.
Stay awake and aware.
Be present.
Joy arises from following your soul's intention.
The journey is joy.
Stay awake and aware.
Nurture that joy.
The mind prefers comfort.
Beware.
Let go.
Let go again.
Feel the joy of creating,
Of letting the Universe bring that intention to life in creative ways.
Be present.
Breathe.
Listen to your inner guidance.
Tune into your next step.
Take this step now.
Trust.

Let go.

Take the step.

The next one will reveal itself.

Feel the joy of being guided.

Nature takes the most efficient route.

Celebrate the unfolding.

Everything is emerging now.

Feel the joy of creation.

Be the joy.

You are a creation.

You are a creator.

Stay awake and aware.

Love is the material of creation.

Joy is the result.

You are a creation and you are a creator.

You were created from love.

Create with love.

Love your creations.

Love yourself.

Be love.

You are love.

Allow yourself to have this experience.

Allow yourself to be love.

Allow love.

Love.

APPENDIX OF CHARTS

Chart A: Bodygraph

Chart B: Bodygraph with Centers

Chart C: Jackie's Chart

Chart D: Maggie's Chart

Chart E: Sarah's Chart

Chart F: Patty's Chart

Chart G: Barbara's Chart

Chart H: Chart of the 5 Types

Chart I: Patrick's Chart

Chart J: Theresa's Chart

Chart K: Hannah's Chart

CHART A: BODYGRAPH

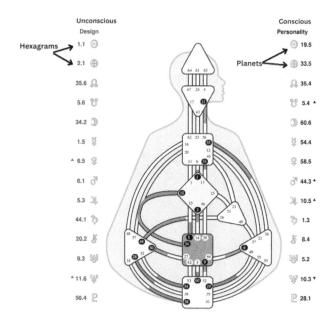

Unconscious
Design

Conscious
Personality

Hexagrams

Planets

Unconscious (Design)	Conscious (Personality)
1.1 ☉	☉ 19.5
2.1 ⊕	⊕ 33.5
35.6 ☊	☊ 35.4
5.6 ☋	☋ 5.4 ▲
34.2 ☽	☽ 60.6
1.5 ☿	☿ 54.4
▲ 6.5 ♀	♀ 58.5
6.1 ♂	♂ 44.3 ▲
5.3 ♃	♃ 10.5 ▲
44.1 ♄	♄ 1.3
20.2 ♅	♅ 8.4
9.3 ♆	♆ 5.2
▲ 11.6 ♇	♇ 10.3 ▼
50.4 ♇	♇ 28.1

CHART B: CENTERS

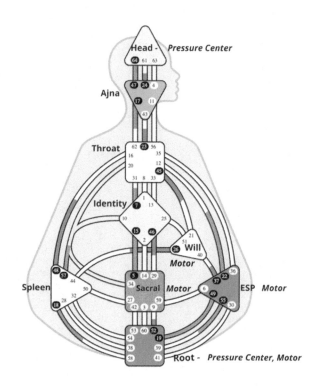

CHART C: JACKIE'S CHART

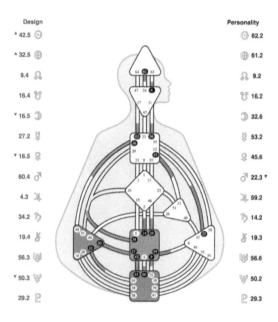

Design		Personality	
▲ 42.5 ☉		☉ 62.2	
▲ 32.5 ⊕		⊕ 61.2	
9.4 ☊		☊ 9.2	
16.4 ☋		☋ 16.2	
▼ 16.5 ☽		☽ 32.6	
27.2 ☿		☿ 53.2	
▼ 16.5 ♀		♀ 45.6	
60.4 ♂		♂ 22.3 ▼	
4.3 ♃		♃ 59.2	
34.2 ♄		♄ 14.2	
19.4 ♅		♅ 19.3	
56.3 ♆		♆ 56.6	
▼ 50.3 ♇		♇ 50.2	
29.2 ♇		♇ 29.3	

Type: Pure Generator
Profile: 2/5 – Hermit/ Heretic
Definition: Single
Inner Authority: Sacral
Strategy: Respond
Incarnation Cross: RAX Maya 2

CHART D: MAGGIE'S CHART

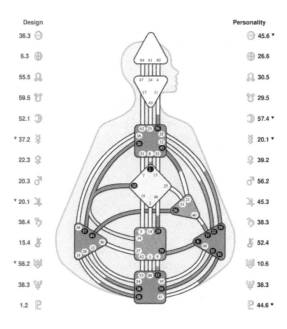

Design			Personality
36.3	☉	☉	45.6 ▼
6.3	⊕	⊕	26.6
55.5	♌	♌	30.5
59.5	☋	☋	29.5
52.1	☽	☽	57.4 ▼
▼ 37.2	☿	☿	20.1 ▼
22.3	♀	♀	39.2
20.3	♂	♂	56.2
▼ 20.1	♃	♃	45.3
38.4	♄	♄	38.3
15.4	♅	♅	52.4
▼ 58.2	♆	♆	10.6
38.3	♇	♇	38.3
1.2	ℙ	ℙ	44.6 *

Type: Emotional Manifesting Generator
Profile: 6/3 – Role Model/ Martyr
Definition: Small Split (12, 18, 28, 34, 35, 40, 46)
Inner Authority: Solar Plexus
Strategy: Respond
Incarnation Cross: LAX Confrontation 1

CHART E: SARAH'S CHART

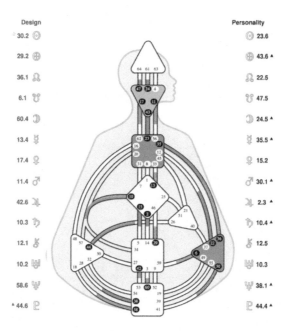

Design		Personality
30.2		23.6
29.2		43.6 ▲
36.1		22.5
6.1		47.5
60.4		24.5 ▲
13.4		35.5 ▲
17.4		15.2
11.4		30.1 ▲
42.6		2.3 ▲
10.3		10.4 ▲
12.1		12.5
10.2		10.3
58.6		38.1 ▲
▲ 44.6		44.4 ▲

Type: Emotional Manifestor
Profile: 6/2 Role Model/ Hermit
Definition: Single
Inner Authority: Solar Plexus
Strategy: Inform and Initiate
Incarnation Cross: LAX Dedication 1

CHART F: PATTY'S CHART

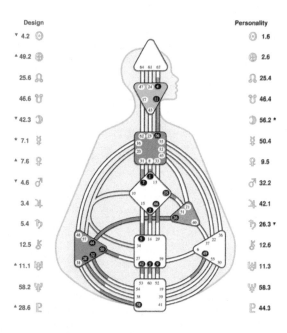

Design		Personality	
▼ 4.2	☉	☉	1.6
▲ 49.2	⊕	⊕	2.6
25.6	♌	♌	25.4
46.6	♉	♉	46.4
▼ 42.3	☽	☽	56.2 *
* 7.1	☿	☿	50.4
▲ 7.6	♀	♀	9.5
▼ 4.6	♂	♂	32.2
3.4	♃	♃	42.1
5.4	♄	♄	26.3 ▼
12.5	♅	♅	12.6
▲ 11.1	♆	♆	11.3
58.2	♇	♇	58.3
▲ 28.6	♇	♇	44.3

Type: Splenic Projector
Profile: 6/2 Role Model / Hermit
Definition: Split – Large
Inner Authority: Splenic
Strategy: Wait for Recognition and Invitation
Incarnation Cross: LAX Defiance 2

CHART G: BARBARA'S CHART

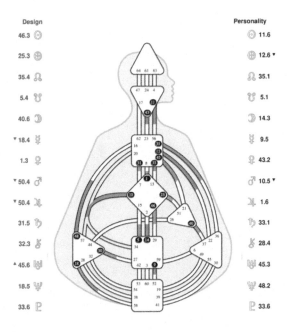

Design		Personality	
46.3	☉	☉	11.6
25.3	⊕	⊕	12.6 ▾
35.4	♌	♌	35.1
5.4	☊	☊	5.1
40.6	☽	☽	14.3
▾ 18.4	☿	☿	9.5
1.3	♀	♀	43.2
▾ 50.4	♂	♂	10.5 ▾
▾ 50.4	♃	♃	1.6
31.5	♄	♄	33.1
32.3	♅	♅	28.4
▴ 45.6	♆	♆	45.3
18.5	♇	♇	48.2
33.6	♇	♇	33.6

Type: Reflector
Profile: 6/3 Role Model / Martyr
Definition: None
Inner Authority: No Inner Authority
Strategy: Wait a Lunar Cycle
Incarnation Cross: LAX Education 2

CHART H: THE FIVE TYPES

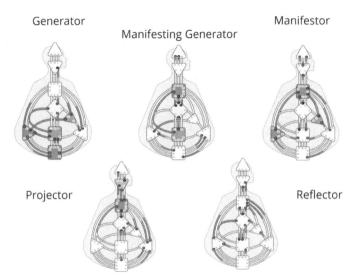

Generator

Manifesting Generator

Manifestor

Projector

Reflector

CHART I: PATRICK'S CHART

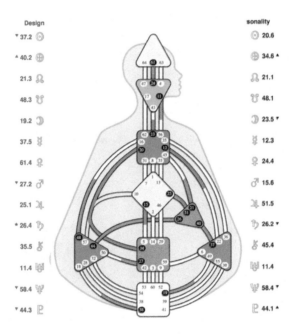

Design		sonality	
▼ 37.2	◉	◉	20.6
▲ 40.2	⊕	⊕	34.6 ▲
21.3	♌	♌	21.1
48.3	♈	♈	48.1
19.2	☽	☽	23.5 ▼
37.5	☿	☿	12.3
61.4	♀	♀	24.4
▼ 27.2	♂	♂	15.6
25.1	♃	♃	51.5
✱ 26.4	♄	♄	26.2 ▼
35.5	♅	♅	45.4
11.4	♆	♆	11.4
▼ 58.4	♇	♇	58.4 ▼
▼ 44.3	♇	♇	44.1 ▲

Type: Emotional Manifesting Generator
Profile: 6/2 – Role Model / Hermit
Definition: Triple Split
Inner Authority: Solar Plexus
Strategy: Respond
Incarnation Cross: LAX Duality 1

CHART J: THERESA'S CHART

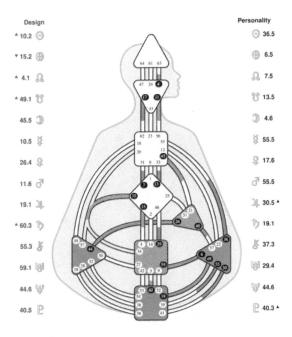

Design		Personality	
▲ 10.2	☉	☉	36.5
▼ 15.2	⊕	⊕	6.5
▲ 4.1	☊	☊	7.5
▲ 49.1	☋	☋	13.5
45.5	☽	☽	4.6
10.5	☿	☿	55.5
26.4	♀	♀	17.6
11.6	♂	♂	55.5
19.1	♃	♃	30.5 ▲
▲ 60.3	♄	♄	19.1
55.3	♇	♇	37.3
59.1	♅	♅	29.4
44.6	♆	♆	44.6
40.5	♇	♇	40.3 ▲

Type: Emotional Generator
Profile: 5/2 – Heretical / Hermit
Definition: Split Small (37)
Inner Authority: Solar Plexus
Strategy: Respond
Incarnation Cross: LAX The Plane 1

CHART K: HANNAH'S CHART

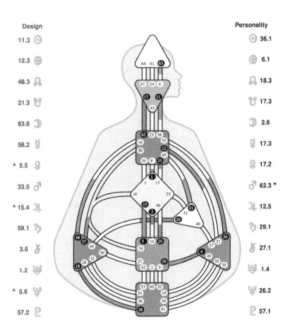

Design	Personality
11.3 ☉	☉ 36.1
12.3 ⊕	⊕ 6.1
48.3 ☊	☊ 18.3
21.3 ☋	☋ 17.3
63.6 ☽	☽ 2.6
58.2 ☿	☿ 17.3
▲ 5.5 ♀	♀ 17.2
33.5 ♂	♂ 62.3 ▾
▲ 15.4 ♃	♃ 12.5
59.1 ♄	♄ 29.1
3.6 ♅	♅ 27.1
1.2 ♆	♆ 1.4
▲ 5.6 ♇	♇ 26.2
57.2 ♇	♇ 57.1

Type: Emotional Generator
Profile: 1/3 – Investigator / Martyr
Definition: Triple Split
Inner Authority: Solar Plexus
Strategy: Respond
Incarnation Cross: RAX Eden 1

ADDITIONAL APPENDICES

APPENDIX A: RESOURCES FOR A DEEPER DIVE INTO HUMAN DESIGN

BOOKS BY ROBIN WINN

- *Understanding Your Clients Through Human Design: The Breakthrough Technology*
- *Understanding the Centers in Human Design: The Facilitator's Guide to Transforming Pain into Possibility*
- *Understanding the Profiles: The Facilitator's Guide to Unleashing Potential*

BOOK BY CHETAN PARKYN AND CAROLA EASTWOOD

- *The Book of Destinies*

OTHER BOOKS BY KRISTIN PANEK

- *My Family Needs My Spiritual Leadership Now: The Guide to Being Your Family's Spiritual Support*
- *Authentic Leadership: The Guide to Be a Spiritual Leader in Your Community*

LINK TO GENERATE YOUR HUMAN DESIGN CHART

- www.LeadbyDesignwithKristin.com/bodygraph

For a session to review your Human Design chart, contact Kristin at KristinPanek@gmail.com.

APPENDIX B: SURFACING BELIEFS PROCESS

Close your eyes.
Breathe deeply and slowly.
Bring to mind a situation that still triggers you.
Start at the beginning and observe this situation unfolding, as if it's happening now.
Breathe.
Observe without judgment and without resistance.
When you reach the point in this situation where you feel a disturbance or reaction, direct your attention to where you feel it in the body.
It may show up as an emotion, or a pain or other sensation.
Place your full attention on that sensation in your body.
Let go of any resistance to feeling.
Relax your breathing but keep your attention focused in that area.
Let go of thoughts.
Observe the sensation without intensifying it.
Let go of the story of this situation.
Keep returning your attention to the sensation.
Breathe slowly.
If the sensation moves to another part of the body, follow it.
Keep your attention focused on the most intense point of sensation.
Observe.
Breathe slowly
Memories may surface.
Observe them without attachment.
Keep attention focused on the strongest sensation.
Older memories may surface.
Breathe slowly.
You may feel you're going back in time.
Back to your childhood through this sensation.
All the way back.
Don't think about it.

Breathe.

How old are you and what is happening for you?

Accept whatever impression you get.

What are you as a child, saying to yourself?

Listen.

Maybe you are saying:

They don't listen to me.

They don't like me.

I'm in trouble.

Look at what you as a child are saying.

As you see yourself saying it,

inhale and hold your breath for as long as you can.

Release.

Let it all go.

Breathe deeply.

You may feel lightness coming in.

You may already feel a release of energy around the situation.

Breathe.

Breathe in self forgiveness.

Release any judgment on the outbreath.

Breathe in forgiveness of others in this situation.

Breathe out any remnants of that experience.

Feel gratitude for any insights received.

Open your eyes.

Write any insights in your journal. You might begin to see more places where this belief or this experience has impacted your life. Practice this one as many times as it takes to get comfortable with the process and to see the truth. As Sri Bhagavan says, "To see is to be free."

APPENDIX C: RELEASING THE ENERGY BEHIND THE CHARGE PROCESS

This is simple, but it requires attention and focus.

Close your eyes. Take three deep, slow breaths.
Connect in your heart with your Divine.
Ask for support in releasing charges.
Find an interaction from today that hurt you.
It doesn't matter how small the incident.
Place yourself in the situation as if it is happening now.
As it unfolds, let go of the stories in the mind and place all of your attention on whatever feeling arises.
You will likely feel this somewhere in the body.
Place your focus there and stay present with it.
Keep opening into the feeling without making it bigger or holding on to it.
Breathe.
Keep releasing any stories your mind is producing.
Keep focusing your attention.
You may receive an old memory or a belief.
See that memory or belief and keep feeling.
You'll know when the energy behind it starts to release.
Stay with it until it is complete.
Give gratitude to the Divine for the support.

This is a great way to end each day. Look for any pain you've received from interactions with others and release the charges.
Excerpt from *My Family Needs My Leadership Now.*

APPENDIX D: FULL-LENGTH MEDITATION TO SURFACE BELIEFS IN THE CENTERS

While there are certain themes associated with each Center, don't limit yourself to that. In this meditation, relax into your experience of the Center and let it inform you. I may provide an example, but trust the impressions you receive and be sure to enjoy the process.

Sit comfortably in a quiet space and close your eyes.
Focus on your breathing as you take three deep inhales and slow exhales.
Bring your goal to mind.
Say your goal out loud to yourself.
Your intention is to surface the beliefs that are in the way of your goal.
Ask for support from your higher self to see this.
Inhale deeply, exhale slowly.
With your attention inside yourself, open your eyes and look at your chart.
Take a deep breath and imagine this chart is alive inside you.
Locate your Head Center, noting if it's Defined or Open.
Inhale deeply and sense its presence in your head.
Exhale slowly.
Move your attention to the Ajna Center.
Inhale deeply and sense its presence in your head.
Exhale slowly.
Continue with the remaining seven Centers.
Inhaling, sensing each one's presence, and exhaling slowly.
Don't worry about getting it right.
Get an impression of where it is in your body and accept whatever impression you get.
When you're complete, keep your eyes closed.
Relax your breathing and sense the entire bodygraph inside.
Align with your intention to surface sabotaging beliefs.
Now tune back in to your Head Center.

With your focus on this Center, say your goal statement out loud.
Observe any thoughts that arise in conflict with that statement.
For example: "I'm not ready."
Or: "I need more information."
Watch the thoughts that are triggered by the statement of your goal.
Whichever thought has the most energy behind it, write that down.
Bring attention to the sensation attached to the thought.
Breathe and focus your attention on the sensation without intensifying it.
Let it be.
Let go of any other thoughts that arise as you keep your focus here.
If the sensation moves, follow it with your full attention.
Breathe and relax the body.
If memories surface, see them and let them go.
When the sensation releases or drops in intensity, then breathe.
Listen for any message from your Head Center.
Write that down.
What thought or belief would you like to create in place of the one you released?
It may be based on the message you received, or it may be different.
For example, if the thought was "I'm not ready," you could substitute,
"I'm ready to act as soon as my inner guidance gives me direction."
Tune in to a helpful belief for your situation.
Then write it down.
Say that belief out loud.
Then listen. If you receive guidance, write that down too.
Close your eyes and breathe deeply.
Align with your intention to surface sabotaging beliefs.
Now tune back into your Ajna Center.
With your focus on this Center, say your goal statement out loud.
Observe any thoughts that arise in conflict with that statement.
For example: "I'm not certain," or "I know what's best but they don't take my advice."
Watch the thoughts that are triggered by the statement of your goal, without judgment.
Whichever thought has the most energy behind it, write that down.
Bring attention to the sensation attached to the thought.
Breathe and focus your attention on the sensation without intensifying it.
Let it be.
Let go of any other thoughts that arise as you keep your focus here.
If the sensation moves, follow it with your full attention.
Breathe and relax the body.
If memories surface, see them and let them go
When the sensation releases or drops in intensity, then breathe.

Listen for any message from your Ajna Center
Write that down.
What thought or belief would you like to create in place of the one you released?
It may be based on the message you received, or it may be different.
For example, if the thought was "I'm not certain and I need to be,"
you could substitute, "I am a witness. Whatever I need is given to me when I need it."
Tune in to a helpful belief for your situation.
Then write it down.
Say that belief out loud.
Then listen. If you receive guidance, write that down too.
Close your eyes and breathe deeply.
Align with your intention to surface sabotaging beliefs.
Now tune back in to your Throat Center.
With your focus on this Center say your goal statement out loud.
Observe any thoughts that arise in conflict with that statement.
For example: "No one listens to me."
Watch the thoughts that are triggered by the statement of your goal, without judgment.
Whichever thought has the most energy behind it, write that down.
Bring attention to the sensation attached to the thought.
Breathe and focus your attention on the sensation without intensifying it.
Let it be.
Let go of any other thoughts that arise as you keep your focus here.
If the sensation moves, follow it with your full attention.
Breathe and relax the body.
If memories surface, see them and let them go.
When the sensation releases or drops in intensity, then breathe.
Listen for any message from your Throat Center.
Write that down.
What thought or belief would you like to create in place of the one you released?
It may be based on the message you received, or it may be different.
For example, if the thought was "No one listens to me," you could substitute,
"I follow my Strategy and Authority regarding when to speak and to whom."
Tune in to a helpful belief for your situation.
Then write it down.
Say that belief out loud.
Then listen. If you receive guidance, write that down too.
Close your eyes and breathe deeply.
Align with your intention to surface sabotaging beliefs.
Now tune back in to your Identity Center.
With your focus on this Center, say your goal statement out loud.
Observe any thoughts that arise in conflict with that statement.

For example: "I feel like an imposter," or "I know the way, but they won't follow."
Watch the thoughts that are triggered by the statement of your goal, without judgment.
Whichever thought has the most energy behind it, write that down.
Bring attention to the sensation attached to the thought.
Breathe and focus your attention on the sensation without intensifying it.
Let it be.
Let go of any other thoughts that arise as you keep your focus here.
If the sensation moves, follow it with your full attention.
Breathe and relax the body.
If memories surface, see them and let them go.
When the sensation releases or drops in intensity, then breathe.
Listen for any message from your Identity Center.
Write that down.
What thought or belief would you like to create in place of the one you released?
It may be based on the message you received, or it may be different.
For example, if the thought was "I feel like an imposter,"
you could substitute, "Whoever I am in this moment is perfect."
Tune in to a helpful belief for your situation.
Then write it down.
Say that belief out loud.
Then listen. If you receive guidance, write that down too.
Close your eyes and breathe deeply.
Align with your intention to surface sabotaging beliefs.
Now tune back into your Will Center.
With your focus on this Center, say your goal statement out loud
Observe any thoughts that arise in conflict with that statement.
For example: "I should do what I say I'm going to do,"
or "They should meet their deadlines."
Watch the thoughts that are triggered by the statement of your goal, without judgment.
Whichever thought has the most energy behind it, write that down.
Bring attention to the sensation attached to the thought.
Breathe and focus your attention on the sensation without intensifying it.
Let it be.
Let go of any other thoughts that arise as you keep your focus here.
If the sensation moves, follow it with your full attention.
Breathe and relax the body.
If memories surface, see them and let them go
When the sensation releases or drops in intensity, then breathe.
Listen for any message from your Will Center.
Write that down.

What thought or belief would you like to create in place of the one you released?
It may be based on the message you received, or it may be different.
For example, if the thought was "I should do what I say,"
you could substitute, "I know my value."
Tune in to a helpful belief for your situation.
Then write it down.
Say that belief out loud.
Then listen. If you receive guidance, write that down too.
Close your eyes and breathe deeply.
Align with your intention to surface sabotaging beliefs.
Now tune back into your Sacral Center.
With your focus on this Center, say your goal statement out loud.
Observe any thoughts that arise in conflict with that statement.
For example: "I should have more energy," or "They should work at least as hard as I do."
Watch the thoughts that are triggered by the statement of your goal, without judgment.
Whichever thought has the most energy behind it, write that down.
Bring attention to the sensation attached to the thought.
Breathe and focus your attention on the sensation without intensifying it.
Let it be.
Let go of any other thoughts that arise as you keep your focus here.
If the sensation moves, follow it with your full attention.
Breathe and relax the body.
If memories surface, see them and let them go
When the sensation releases or drops in intensity, then breathe.
Listen for any message from your Sacral Center
Write that down.
What thought or belief would you like to create in place of the one you released?
It may be based on the message you received, or it may be different.
For example, if the thought was "I should have more energy,"
you could substitute, "I honor my body and enjoy resting and rejuvenating as needed."
Tune in to a helpful belief for your situation.
Then write it down.
Say that belief out loud.
Then listen. If you receive guidance, write that down too.
Close your eyes and breathe deeply.
Align with your intention to surface sabotaging beliefs.
Now tune back in to your Root Center.
With your focus on this Center, say your goal statement out loud.
Observe any thoughts that arise in conflict with that statement.
For example: "I should do something," or "They should do something."

Watch the thoughts that are triggered by the statement of your goal, without judgment.

Whichever thought has the most energy behind it, write that down.

Bring attention to the sensation attached to the thought.

Breathe and focus your attention on the sensation without intensifying it.

Let it be.

Let go of any other thoughts that arise as you keep your focus here.

If the sensation moves, follow it with your full attention.

Breathe and relax the body.

If memories surface, see them and let them go.

When the sensation releases or drops in intensity, then breathe.

Listen for any message from your Root Center.

Write that down.

What thought or belief would you like to create in place of the one you released?

It may be based on the message you received, or it may be different.

For example, if the thought was "I should do something,"

you could substitute, "I discern what is mine to do based on my Strategy and Authority."

Tune in to a helpful belief for your situation.

Then write it down.

Say that belief out loud.

Then listen. If you receive guidance, write that down too.

Close your eyes and breathe deeply.

Align with your intention to surface sabotaging beliefs.

Now tune back in to your Emotional Solar Plexus.

With your focus on this Center, say your goal statement out loud.

Observe any thoughts that arise in conflict with that statement.

For example: "I shouldn't be so unfeeling," or "I shouldn't feel that way."

Watch the thoughts that are triggered by the statement of your goal, without judgment.

Whichever thought has the most energy behind it, write that down.

Bring attention to the sensation attached to the thought.

Breathe and focus your attention on the sensation without intensifying it.

Let it be.

Let go of any other thoughts that arise as you keep your focus here.

If the sensation moves, follow it with your full attention.

Breathe and relax the body.

If memories surface, see them and let them go

When the sensation releases or drops in intensity, then breathe.

Listen for any message from your Emotional Solar Plexus.

Write that down.

What thought or belief would you like to create in place of the one you released?

It may be based on the message you received, or it may be different.
For example, if the thought was "I shouldn't be so unfeeling,"
you could substitute, "I honor what I am feeling or not feeling in the moment."
Tune into a helpful belief for your situation.
Then write it down.
Say that belief out loud.
Then listen. If you receive guidance, write that down too.
Close your eyes and breathe deeply.
Align with your intention to surface sabotaging beliefs.
Now tune back in to your Spleen
With your focus on this Center, say your goal statement out loud.
Observe any thoughts that arise in conflict with that statement.
For example: "I shouldn't be so afraid," or "I'm always late."
Watch the thoughts that are triggered by the statement of your goal, without judgment.
Whichever thought has the most energy behind it, write that down.
Bring attention to the sensation attached to the thought.
Breathe and focus your attention on the sensation without intensifying it.
Let it be.
Let go of any other thoughts that arise as you keep your focus here.
If the sensation moves, follow it with your full attention.
Breathe and relax the body.
If memories surface, see them and let them go
When the sensation releases or drops in intensity, then breathe.
Listen for any message from your Spleen.
Write that down.
What thought or belief would you like to create in place of the one you released?
It may be based on the message you received, or it may be different.
For example, if the thought was "I shouldn't be so afraid,"
you could substitute, "I'm alert and aware in the present moment."
Tune in to a helpful belief for your situation.
Then write it down.
Say that belief out loud.
Then listen. If you receive guidance, write that down too.

APPENDIX E: HANDLING SABOTAGING BELIEF PROCESS

Start with a belief that surfaced that needs to be released.

Close your eyes and breathe.

When you hold that belief, where in the body (not head) do you feel it?

That belief triggers a feeling (how it got lodged in your system in an infinite loop).

The feeling is a reaction to the belief that moves you into action

You take action and this causes a repeating situation that disturbs your peace.

Now, let's release the energy behind it so the belief is not running in your subconscious.

To release it, hold focus and allow the feeling to move.

Keep your focus steady and relax everything else. Release any resistance.

The energy will release.

You may get a partial release or full one (if partial, do this again later).

Now that there is some relief, let's look more closely at this belief.

See all the areas in your life where it's operating.

This program is constantly running, so find all the places it shows up.

Look over the landscape of your life and the impact of running this belief.

Acknowledge that you took on this belief.

You created the belief and the resulting impact that you are seeing before you.

To shift it you must take ownership.

A creation like this needs energy to keep running.

It's using your energy.

See how you are still feeding it energy.

Pause.

Now that you've seen this belief, owned it, and released the excess energy, you can decide to drop it – turn it off.

Stop giving it your energy. Let it go.

Pause.

Now there's an empty space in your consciousness.

Write down a new belief – a reality you prefer.

Post it somewhere you will see it.

If the old belief arises again, stop and replace it with the new one.
Say the new belief to yourself.
Start to notice the feelings that arise from the new belief and what actions you take.
Write those down in a journal so you can start to see the impact of the new belief.
Once your mind sees the benefit of replacing the old belief for the new one, it will help you.

If this belief still doesn't release, I recommend using Byron Katie's inquiry process to work on it. Her website is: www.thework.com. Here is the link to the worksheets with instructions: https://thework.com/instruction-the-work-byron-katie/

APPENDIX F: LETTING GO PROCESS

Use this process periodically to train yourself not to hold on to thoughts and feelings:

Close your eyes.
Take a deep breath and release it fast.
Breathe in.
Create tension in the body.
Everywhere in the body.
Tense your toes, legs, torso, arms, fingers, neck, head, face.
Magnify the tension and hold your breath.
Hold it.
Hold it.
Let go.
Inhale deeply.
Bring in tension from anything you're holding – fears, anger, frustration.
Tense your whole body from your head to your toes.
Hold it.
Hold it
Hold it.
Let go.
Now move into deep inhale and exhale.
Slow it down.
Letting go is as natural as exhaling.
Feel that natural rhythm.
Resisting whatever is happening, stops the breath.
Breathe slowly and deeply.
Now bring to mind something that causes you fear –
fear of the future, of rejection of failure.
See the fear and notice the constriction in the body.
Feel the holding on, the grasping.

Feel the shallow exhale and inhale.

Take a breath.

Now, relax the body.

The fear is just a thought.

See it.

Let it go.

Return to an easy slow breath – inhale and exhale.

Bring to mind a situation where you're trying to control someone or something.

Feel the tension caused by the need to control.

Relax the body.

Is it possible to control someone else?

Is it possible to control your current environment or the weather?

Shift your perspective.

Return to the breath.

Deep inhale, slow exhale.

Bring to mind a story of how someone hurt you.

Feel the hurt in the body.

Allow the sensations to be there.

Take a breath.

Let go of the story.

Breathe slowly.

Allow forgiveness by letting go of the hurt.

Return to the breath.

Bring to mind something or someone you're attached to.

Feel the places where you are grasping, where you're holding on, afraid to lose them.

Notice your breathing right now.

Relax the body.

Take a slow, deep breath.

Let go into love.

Take a breath.

Let go again.

Feel the space you've created.

Tune in to the silence.

Breathe.

What in your life is calling you?

What is that still small voice saying to you?

Receive whatever impressions you get.

Express gratitude.

As you open your eyes, keep some of your attention inside as you tune back in to your world

ACKNOWLEDGMENTS

I would never have written this book if I hadn't experienced such a powerful connection to the Human Design system through Robin Winn. She fully embodies this work and transmits the essence of the teachings in a way that her students can embody it as well. I am deeply grateful for her profound mentorship and for her insightful comments and suggestions as I was writing.

The inspiration for this book arose on a call I attended to support her in encouraging others to write their own books on Human Design. The title and the general gist of this book came to me in a flash. I was surprised by the impulse and received strong encouragement by Robin as well as by Angela Lauria at The Author Incubator to honor that calling. I'm so grateful for their support and for this journey because I have learned so much in the process.

Thank you to my Human Design mastermind group – Heidi, Charlotte, Lauren, Cari and Kelly, who have offered words of encouragement and inspiration along the way. They have helped me anchor in this work more deeply. Thanks also to my other long-term classmates – Moudi, Anna, Iris and Denise, whose insights expanded my understanding of what's possible in working with Human Design charts.

I'm grateful for all the classmates in the various Human Design trainings I've attended, assisted and facilitated. I've learned so much about how other Types of people can more effectively work with their wiring. Thank you to Cari who helped me get the bodygraph software up and running on the website! Your focus, expertise and willingness are greatly appreciated. Thank you to the BodyGraphChart.com team, especially Gytis and Algis who responded quickly to my calls for help in getting software to do what I needed. Huge gratitude to John at Genetic Matrix for your software that makes it easier to create and manage the charts from all my clients.

My Lead by Design_clients and trainees have trusted me to lead them through their various challenges and to reach for their dream goals. Thank you so much for adding joy and deep meaning to this journey.

I am also hugely grateful for the experience of being a part of The Author Incubator. Angela's genius supports authors in moving through their internal obstacles to put their work out in the world. I'm grateful for the comprehensive editing support I've received from Cory, who is also a fantastic cheerleader. I was surprised when so much of the book ended up being a dialogue and was a little nervous about this format. He kept encouraging me to do more. Thank you!

I'm so grateful for Harmony's encouragement, and for her invitation to be on staff at the Harmonic Egg in Naperville. I have enjoyed working with the leaders that have come through her business.

To the Flowering Heart Center Board – Denise, Leenie, Mike, Patrick and Will, who have stood by me through some major changes at our Center – thank you for your continued enthusiasm, support and encouragement. You've been holding the space while I've been focused on this project. Thank you to the Flowering Heart Center community! You kept showing up and drawing the information out of me, which became the basis for this book. I am grateful for your dedication to your own growth process.

Thanks to Dawn, who is responsible for drawing me out

onto the El Camino way twice in three years. This time we walked while I was in the middle of writing this book, and I appreciate your open heart, encouragement, and words of wisdom. I look forward to more travels with you.

Thank you to Kay for creating a beautiful cover for this book. I appreciate your artistry and your patience with my process.

I'm grateful for my weekly calls with author and friend, Catherine. You were the catalyst for writing my first book and for inspiring me to write the second one. Thanks for always speaking just the right words to bring me to a place of Inner Peace.

Thank you to my children who continue to show me who I am. I'm grateful for their love and support. To my new grandson Jack, whose very existence gave me a new name – Gamma!

Huge gratitude to my ancestors who were with me on this journey too. I uncovered old photos and letters from my parents and grandparents and learned that they were writers too. My mother's teacher was encouraging her to write a book about her story. My dad even won a limerick contest in 1949 and received an all-expense paid trip to New York!

To my beloved husband Frank, who has always been there for me through the twists and turns of this particular journey. Thank you for your deep abiding love, for your editing expertise, your wisdom and for your artist's eye.

To Dr. Lawrence, my spiritual mentor, who has helped me become more fully embodied so that I can offer more to others. I'm so grateful for your support and for the vastness of the Being that you are.

Huge gratitude to all of my teachers and all of the trainings I've received. The concepts I've been working with around creating reality for over twenty years are anchored in the Avatar materials, Shematrix mystery school, Oneness University, The Work of Byron Katie, trainings with Sonia Choquette, Atma Nambi, David Hawkins and many more. The *Reality Transurfing* materials have inspired me to take things to another level. Each of these teachers and their teachings have touched me on a deep level and have expanded my idea of what's possible.

I have the highest gratitude and appreciation for my Spirit guides who are the real authors of this book. I witness the material flowing through and the grace that rides along with it. Thank you for the inspiration and the creation of this book. It was a consuming and joyful process.

May you, the reader, receive the full transmission of this work and get a glimpse of what's possible when you Lead by Design.

ABOUT THE AUTHOR

Kristin Panek is the bestselling author of *Authentic Leadership: The Guide to be a Spiritual Leader in Your Community* and *My Family Needs My Spiritual Leadership Now: The Guide to Being Your Family's Spiritual Support*. Kristin combines the best of two decades of business experience with over two decades of spiritual work to bring you an innovative way to work with your Human Design to strengthen your leadership skills.

Kristin is the founder and spiritual director of Flowering Heart Center (FHC), a not-for-profit in Oak Brook, Illinois. After twenty years in a successful management career at Ameritech, Kristin left to pursue transformational work with Shematrix, involving Rites of Initiation into the Divine Feminine. While facilitating this work and receiving extensive training in India for twenty years, she founded FHC to support community healing and transformation into higher states of consciousness.

Kristin is an ordained interfaith minister of the Seraphic Order of the Flowering Heart. She is a heart-centered spiritual empowerment mentor, teacher, and international speaker. By transforming deeply rooted beliefs and fostering the connection to the Divine within, she supports a diverse group of leaders on their awakening path to step into their fullest potential.

She draws on her extensive experience in various modalities including as a facilitator for The Work of Byron Katie, an Avatar master – training in managing consciousness and creating preferred realities, a licensed practitioner by Sonia Choquette – developing intuition, trainer for Oneness – offering various processes for awakening. When she found Human Design, she realized immediately the benefits for her clients and teams and started incorporating it into her work.

As a Human Design consultant and facilitator, Kristin brings a unique perspective, supporting her clients to dive deeply into their design and to appreciate their unique wiring and how it will lead them toward their goals. Her clients feel empowered and gain a deeper understanding and reverence for their true selves.

She lives in the Chicago area with her beloved husband Frank.

ABOUT DIFFERENCE PRESS

Difference Press is the publishing arm of The Author Incubator, an Inc. 500 award-winning company that helps business owners and executives grow their brand, establish thought leadership, and get customers, clients, and highly-paid speaking opportunities, through writing and publishing books.

While traditional publishers require that you already have a large following to guarantee they make money from sales to your existing list, our approach is focused on using a book to grow your following – even if you currently don't have a following. This is why we charge an up-front fee but never take a percentage of revenue you earn from your book.

☞ MORE THAN A COACH. MORE THAN A PUBLISHER. ✍

We work intimately and personally with each of our authors to develop a revenue-generating strategy for the book. By using a Lean Startup style methodology, we guarantee the book's success before we even start writing. We provide all the technical support authors need with editing, design, marketing, and publishing, the emotional support you would get from a book coach to help you manage anxiety and time constraints, and we serve as a strategic thought partner engineering the book for success.

The Author Incubator has helped almost 2,000 entrepreneurs write, publish, and promote their non-fiction books. Our authors have used their books to gain international media exposure, build a brand and marketing following, get lucrative speaking engagements, raise awareness of their product or service, and attract clients and customers.

☞ ARE YOU READY TO WRITE A BOOK? ✍

As a client, we will work with you to make sure your book gets done right and that it gets done quickly. The Author Incubator provides one-stop for strategic book consultation, author coaching to manage writer's block and anxiety, full-service professional editing, design, and self-publishing services, and book marketing and launch campaigns. We sell this as one package so our clients are not slowed down with contradictory advice. We have a 99 percent success rate with nearly all of our clients completing their books, publishing them, and reaching bestseller status upon launch.

☞ APPLY NOW AND BE OUR NEXT SUCCESS STORY ✍

To find out if there is a significant ROI for you to write a book, get on our calendar by completing an application at www.TheAuthorIncubator.com/apply.

OTHER BOOKS BY DIFFERENCE PRESS

Profitable Salon Owner: Rise Above the Chaos In Your Business and Reignite Your Passion and Profits by Jason Everett

Leadership Recreated: A Woman's Guide to Surviving and Thriving in Patriarchal Academia by Kem Gambrell, Ph.D.

Happy Gay Christian Hereafter: 8 Steps to Reconcile Your Identity to Family and Faith or Leave without Regret by Carter Neill Holmes

Talk More, Fight Less: Rebuilding, Renewing, and Restoring Communication in Your Relationship by Dr. Sandra W. Ingram

Starting and Serving: Your Personal Guide to Launching a Successful, New Career as a Nonprofit Leader by R. Romona Jackson, Esq.

The Photographer's Path: Do What You Love, Tell Client's Stories through Images, and Have the Business of Your Dreams by Maya Manseau

Marathon in the Fog: Supporting a Parent with Dementia in Life and Death by Jennifer Olden, LMFT

GIFT FOR THE READER

Thank you dear leader for taking this leadership journey with me. It takes courage to walk this path, to dive deeply into who you are and how you interface with people and situations. I honor your dedication to truth, to excellence, and to making an impact in the world.

There is so much more to learn and discover about your design , your leadership and working with others. If you feel inspired to continue your journey, reach out to me at Kristin Panek@gmail.com.

Meanwhile, if you would like to receive a free copy of the companion video class for Lead by Design or an audio recording of one of the meditations, as a gift for reading my book, contact me at KristinPanek@gmail.com.

Enjoy your learning path!

Blessings,

Kristin

Made in the USA
Las Vegas, NV
07 March 2024

86854832R10138